The Nurse Workforce in the Eastern Caribbean

DIRECTIONS IN DEVELOPMENT
Human Development

The Nurse Workforce in the Eastern Caribbean

Meeting the Challenges of Noncommunicable Diseases

Carmen Carpio and Danielle Fuller-Wimbush

ISBN (paper): 978-1-4648-0830-2
ISBN (electronic): 978-1-4648-0831-9
DOI: 10.1596/978-1-4648-0830-2

Cover photo: © Carmen Carpio. Further permission required for reuse.
Cover design: Debra Naylor, Naylor Design, Washington, DC.

Library of Congress Cataloging-in-Publication Data
Names: Carpio, Carmen, author. | Fuller-Wimbush, Danielle, author. | World
  Bank, publisher.
Title: The nurse workforce in the Eastern Caribbean : meeting the challenges
  of noncommunicable diseases / Carmen Carpio, Danielle Fuller-Wimbush.
Other titles: Directions in development (Washington, D.C.)
Description: Washington, DC : The World Bank, 2016. | Series: Directions in
  development | Includes bibliographical references.
Identifiers: LCCN 2016015273 (print) | LCCN 2016016936 (ebook) | ISBN
  9781464808302 (pdf) | ISBN 9781464808319 | ISBN 9781464808302 (pdf) | ISBN
  9781464808319 ()
Subjects: | MESH: Nursing—manpower | Chronic Disease—prevention & control |
  West Indies
Classification: LCC HD5724 (print) | LCC HD5724 (ebook) | NLM WY 16 DW5 | DDC
  331.13/602461073—dc23
LC record available at https://lccn.loc.gov/2016015273

Contents

Figures

Maps

Tables

Acknowledgments

This study was prepared by the World Bank's Health, Nutrition, and Population Global Practice. Carmen Carpio (Task Team Leader, World Bank) coauthored the study with Danielle Fuller-Wimbush (Consultant). Neesha Harnam (Health Specialist, World Bank) and Selvi Jeyaseelan (Consultant) contributed valuable research inputs. Key World Bank study team members included Elida Caballero Cabrera, Viviana Gonzalez, and Claudia Patricia Pacheco-Flores, who provided logistical and document processing support. Cecilia Parker edited the manuscript, and Evelyn Rodriguez coordinated the study's dissemination and publication process.

For an input to the study, the team commissioned a review of (1) the skill sets, education, and training opportunities of health workers treating noncommunicable diseases, and of (2) policies in the Caribbean governing human resources for health issues.

The study team thanks the officials in the four case study countries— Dominica, Grenada, St. Lucia, and St. Vincent and the Grenadines—who shared with our team the status of human resources for health in their countries.

We acknowledge the work the Pan American Health Organization has done in this region, particularly on developing the Road Map for Strengthening the Caribbean Health Workforce 2012–17. We thank Ian Hambleton, Professor of Biostatistics at the University of the West Indies, for his input and advice, particularly on the study's quantitative components. We also thank the Government of Norway for funding this study.

The team expresses its gratitude to Enis Barış (Practice Manager for the World Bank's Health, Nutrition, and Population Global Practice: Middle East, Haiti, and the Caribbean regions) for his technical guidance in completing this study. The team also acknowledges peer reviewers Akiko Maeda (Lead Health Specialist) and Christophe Lemière (Senior Health Specialist), both with the World Bank's Health, Nutrition, and Population Global Practice, for their technical inputs and suggestions.

About the Authors

Carmen Carpio is a Senior Operations Officer in the World Bank's Global Practice for Health, Nutrition, and Population. She works on health systems strengthening projects across countries in Latin America and the Caribbean and in Sub-Saharan Africa, ranging from upper- and middle-income countries to fragile and conflict states. Her technical experience includes project implementation and analytical work in the areas of public health emergency response, human resources for health, health information systems, surveillance system strengthening, HIV/AIDS, noncommunicable diseases, and nutrition. She holds a Certificate in strengthening human resources for health from Harvard University's School of Public Health, a Master's in public health from the George Washington University, and a Master's from Georgetown University's School of Foreign Service in Latin American economic studies.

Danielle Fuller-Wimbush holds a Ph.D. from the Heller School for Social Policy at Brandeis University in Massachusetts and a Master's in public administration from the University of Southern California. She works as an independent researcher in the field of global health and development, with a focus on results-based financing, human resources for health, sustainable agriculture, and aid effectiveness. Her work has spanned Latin America and the Caribbean, Africa, and the United States.

Executive Summary

The rise in noncommunicable diseases (NCDs) has triggered shifts in the pattern of mortality and morbidity causes throughout the world. If the health workforce is to be able to effectively meet this challenge, it needs to acquire new skills and competencies. In response to changing health conditions, the Caribbean Community (CARICOM), under the leadership of the Pan American Health Organization, developed in 2012 the Road Map for Strengthening the Caribbean Health Workforce 2012–17. The World Bank has long collaborated with CARICOM's English-speaking countries, especially on the nurse workforce, and was well positioned to support the road map's implementation.

Initially, the collaboration between CARICOM and the World Bank produced a comprehensive study in 2009 on nursing education and the labor market for the nurse workforce. This showed both an insufficient supply of nurses to meet the growing demand for health care and significant losses of human capital at multiple points in the market. The study, the first phase of the collaboration, also highlighted the need for a regional approach to better monitor the nurse workforce, improve and expand training capacities, and manage migration. In response to a request from CARICOM governments, the World Bank, in a second phase, conducted a critical review of legal instruments to identify measures that could be put in place to govern a regional approach and actions.

This study, which is part of this ongoing work, aims to support the implementation of the road map by assessing how the capacity of the nurse workforce can be strengthened to respond to the challenges of NCDs. The focus here is on strengthening the nurse workforce, because it constitutes the largest group of health professionals in the Caribbean. Moreover, nurses play a central role in bolstering preventive health services, which are vital for addressing the demographic and epidemiological transitions that have shifted the burden of disease from infectious to chronic conditions.

This study generates knowledge in two critical areas: (1) an understanding of the educational and training opportunities available to nurses to strengthen their capacity to meet NCD challenges, and (2) a policy inventory of human resources for health (HRH). This includes national and subregional policies, as well as legislation that supports improvements in HRH that can help address NCDs. This analysis is based on four case studies conducted in Dominica, Grenada, St. Lucia, and St. Vincent and the Grenadines.

NCD profiles and analyses show that dietary risks and high body mass indexes are common risk factors in these countries, and that ischemic heart disease and strokes are major causes of premature death. For years lived with disability, the patterns are also similar across the case study countries, where major depressive disorders, low back pain, and iron-deficiency anemia lead the list of causes. St. Lucia is the exception because of the loss of life caused by a hurricane in 2010, the data collection year for the Global Burden of Diseases, Injuries, and Risk Factors Study.

The case studies show that nurse staffing levels, in terms of numbers, seem sufficient in all four countries. However, they are dealing with a substantial shortage of specialists, and the management of personnel needs to be strengthened to use staff more effectively. The shortage of specialists is partly because of a lack of in-country training and education opportunities in key specialty areas. At the time of writing, midwifery is the only specialized training offered in the four countries. Moreover, even though they have sufficient numbers of nurses, health clinics still experience staffing shortages. Absenteeism is a major concern in some of the countries, with nurses leaving work early or not showing up at all. Nurses receive generous vacation time and sick leave—upward of 55 days a year. Better personnel management will require penalties for absenteeism, a review of leave policies, and implementation of a staff-scheduling system that ensures hospitals and clinics are adequately covered.

Age gaps in the nurse workforce are an issue in two of the case study countries. The problem here is that many nurses are nearing retirement—and this cohort includes the most skilled nurses. Without a succession plan in place, these countries cannot prepare for replacing the skills and experience of retiring nurses.

While the quality of nursing education is reported to be good overall, there are barriers to accessing specialty training. The Regional Nursing Body sets the curriculum, designs the qualifying exams, and is responsible for standardizing nursing education in the region. All four case study countries have a basic nursing program (either at associate or bachelor level) and midwifery training, but not specialized training. This is mainly offered at the University of the West Indies at its campuses in Barbados, Jamaica, and Trinidad and Tobago. This setup, however, poses a financial burden for many nurses, and requires that families relocate if they do not live in one of the Caribbean countries where specialized nursing programs are offered. And those who pursue specialty training are not given built-in incentives such as automatic pay increases. Thus, high costs, no local opportunities for specialty training, and lack of incentives are causing the shortage of specialists in the case study countries.

This study's findings show that none of the case study countries have developed an HRH policy, though St. Lucia, with the assistance of a consultant from the Commonwealth Secretariat,[1] is in the process of developing one. If successful, it will be the first country in the region to develop an HRH plan. Two of the four countries are working on a strategic plan for health. These efforts, along with a human-resource audit, are essential to guide HRH planning.

None of the four case study countries have a senior-level HRH director or a unit to deal with succession planning and retention policies. Their centralized government structure requires that hiring and firing decisions are made outside ministries of health—in most cases, by a public service commission. Because of this structure, the process for hiring new recruits is slow—and delays in health care, especially if adequate personnel are not in place, can have life and death consequences. Further, the committees making hiring decisions do not always have a clinical background to assess the competency or qualification of applicants. In all four countries, basic human resources needs such as scheduling and vacation planning are handled by junior-level administrative staff. Moreover, not enough champions are in ministries of health to advocate for better HRH policies.

A literature review of legislation and HRH planning and management identified four core planning and six core management components that need to be implemented before further HRH infrastructure can be developed. National plans for health and HRH management units, information systems, and multisectoral taskforces were identified in the literature review as essential components for HRH planning. With respect to management, all four countries need to put in place performance management systems, standardized processes for recruitment, opportunities for continuing professional development or in-service training, plans for monitoring retention, and processes for succession planning.

Ministries of health need to be strengthened to manage staff better and to plan for future staffing needs. Training manuals and written protocols are largely absent. Where they do exist, individual copies are usually not given to nurses and only a hospital copy is available. Most of the four countries lack sophisticated health information system databases and rely on paper records. A database that tracks specialties, skills, and training is lacking in all four countries. St. Lucia is the only one that has started a multisectoral taskforce to engage other sectors on human resources issues.

None of the case study countries has established all four core components for strategic HRH planning. A toolkit—based on the findings of a gap analysis—was developed as part of this study to strengthen the capacity for HRH planning and the management of NCDs.

Note

1. The Commonwealth is an association of 53 independent and equal sovereign states from five regions, most of which were once under the British Crown. The Commonwealth Secretariat provides guidance on policy making and offers technical assistance and advisory services to member countries.

Abbreviations

BMI	body mass index
CCM	chronic care model
CARICOM	Caribbean Community
CARMEN	Collaborative Action for Risk Factor Prevention and Effective Management of NCDs
CCH	Caribbean Cooperation in Health
DALY	disability-adjusted life year
EBP	evidence-based practice
HRH	human resources for health
KACE	Knowledge, Attitudes, Access, and Confidence Evaluation
NCD	noncommunicable disease
PAHO	Pan American Health Organization
PHC	primary health care
USAID	United States Agency for International Development
WHO	World Health Organization
YLDs	years lived with disability
YLLs	years of life lost

CHAPTER 1

Overview of the Eastern Caribbean Health Sector

Introduction

Eastern Caribbean countries have significantly improved the health of their populations since the 1990s. Life expectancy at birth and infant mortality are the two most widely used proxy indicators for assessing the health status of a population, and Eastern Caribbean countries tend to score well on both (table 1.1). Life expectancy in the region ranges from 72.6 years in Grenada to 75.7 years in Antigua and Barbuda, and this compares favorably with life expectancy in what the United Nations defines as "more developed regions" (Australia and New Zealand, Europe, Japan, and North America). According to 2013 World Bank data, infant mortality rates range from 6.1 deaths per 1,000 live births in Antigua and Barbuda to 17.2 deaths in St. Vincent and the Grenadines, broadly in line with the regional average for Latin America and the Caribbean of 15.5 deaths per 1,000 live births.

New Health Challenges and Shortages of Human Resources for Health

Despite these health gains, Eastern Caribbean countries face the new health challenge of an upsurge in noncommunicable diseases (NCDs), which now rank among the major causes of death in the region (table 1.2). Demographic and epidemiological changes, as well as burgeoning urbanization and population aging, caused this shift. NCDs are responsible for four out of five deaths in the region; cardiovascular diseases cause roughly half of these deaths, and cancer causes about one-fifth. Moreover, no region in the world has higher death rates from diabetes mellitus than the Caribbean. The prevalence of people ages 20–79 living with diabetes in the six Eastern Caribbean countries in table 1.2 is estimated to range from a low of 7.1 percent in Antigua and Barbuda to a high of 11.5 percent in Dominica, and no evidence indicates the incidence of diabetes is declining. Major NCDs share underlying risk factors, such as unhealthy eating

Table 1.1 Demographic and Health Indicators, Latest Available Year

	Antigua and Barbuda	Dominica	Grenada	St. Kitts and Nevis	St. Lucia	St. Vincent and the Grenadines
Population	89,985	72,003	105,897	54,000	182,273	109,373
Crude birth rate (per 1,000 population)	16.5	12.8	19.3	12.6	15.4	16.3
Crude death rate (per 1,000 population)	6.1	8.1	7.4	7.5	7.2	7.2
Infant mortality (per 1,000 live births)	7.7	13.9	10.7	13.6	12.7	17.2
Mortality under 5 (per 1,000 live births)	9.3	12.0	11.8	9.0	14.5	19.0
Low birth weight (% <2,500 grams)	5.3	9.4	9.0	9.0	11.2	7.9
Total fertility rate	2.1	1.8	2.2	1.9	1.9	2.0
HALE[a] (years)	64.0	63.0	63.0	63.0	63.0	63.0
Life expectancy at birth (years)	75.7	76.0	72.6	74.4	74.7	73.0
Prevalence of undernourishment (% of population)	22.0	5.0	20.0	14.0	8.0	5.0

Sources: Data from World Bank, WHO, latest available years.
Note: HALE = health-adjusted life expectancy.
a. WHO defines HALE as the average number of years that a person can expect to live in full health by taking into account years lived in less than full health because of disease or injury.

Table 1.2 Age-Standardized DALYs (per 100,000 Population) for Communicable and Selected Noncommunicable Diseases, 2004

Disease type	Antigua and Barbuda	Dominica	Grenada	St. Kitts and Nevis	St. Lucia	St. Vincent and the Grenadines
All cases[a]	16,511	16,395	20,810	18,234	16,329	20,278
Communicable diseases	2,103	2,317	3,582	3,227	2,109	4,128
NCDs						
Selected causes	12,871	12,798	15,601	13,433	11,856	13,828
Malignant neoplasms	1,363	1,768	2,136	1,073	1,333	1,655
Diabetes mellitus	869	629	784	506	915	1,301
Endocrine disorders	694	303	—	672	400	376
Neuropsychiatric conditions	3,554	4,141	3,626	3,713	3,609	3,674
Cardiovascular diseases	2,616	2,117	4,065	3,569	1,849	2,804
Respiratory diseases	750	646	1,169	530	782	833
Digestive diseases	654	691	1,199	702	573	700
Genitourinary diseases	214	241	437	414	200	241
NCDs (%)	78	78	75	74	73	68

Source: WHO data.
Note: — = not available; DALY = disability-adjusted life year; NCD = noncommunicable disease.
a. Including communicable and noncommunicable diseases, and injuries.

habits, physical inactivity, obesity, tobacco and alcohol use, and inadequate use of preventive health services.

NCDs are taking up an increasing portion of health spending. This not only makes it difficult to sustain the current health system, but imposes a large economic burden by, for example, negatively affecting productivity. NCD costs include both the direct costs of individual health expenditures, and indirect costs from earnings losses and the economic burden on families, communities, and public and private health care systems. Spending on diabetes in East Caribbean countries as a percent of total health expenditure ranges from 11 to 15 percent, and the mean annual expenditure per person with diabetes ranges from US$322 to US$769. The annual cost of treating one diabetes case exceeds the annual per capita spending on health by a factor of 1.2 (World Bank 2011). Besides heavy health care expenditures, diabetes weighs on the economy through illness-related lower productivity and lost working days.

NCDs affect men and women differently, and this divergence must be addressed. For example, the prevalence of obesity—a major risk factor for NCDs—is considerably higher among women in Eastern Caribbean countries (figure 1.1). However, alcohol abuse and smoking affect men more than women.

NCDs are no longer diseases of the wealthy; the poor increasingly suffer more NCDs, and the economic burden of these conditions lies most heavily on them. Data from a 2006 St. Lucia household survey show poorer households spent 48 percent of their expenditure per capita on health care, while better-off households spent under 20 percent.

The ability of the Eastern Caribbean states to address NCDs has been further compromised by a shortage of human resources for health (HRH), particularly specialized nurses, which limits the ability of these countries to sustain

Figure 1.1 Prevalence of Obesity (BMI ≥30 kg/m²) Ages 30–100, 2002–15

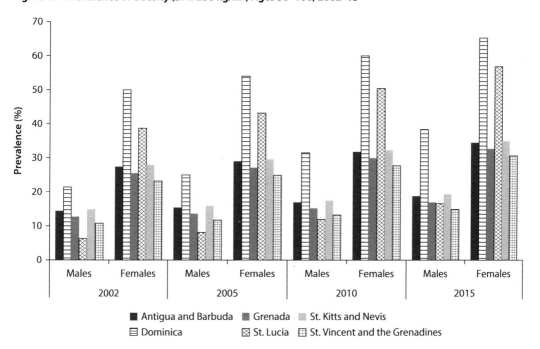

Source: WHO, Global Database on Body Mass Index.
Note: ≥ = greater than or equal to; BMI = body mass index; kg = kilograms; m² = square meters. Data for 2007–09 based on WHO's STEPS framework for surveillance shows lower obesity rates for Dominica: 9 for males and 33 for females in a sample of 1,059 households.

their current health systems and meet their major health service needs. The English-speaking Caribbean countries in particular face an increasing shortage of specialized nurses, who tend to emigrate in large numbers to higher paying jobs in Canada, the United Kingdom, and the United States. This is happening at a time when the demand for quality health care is rising because of population aging. A study of five English-speaking Caribbean countries, which included St. Lucia and St. Vincent and the Grenadines, estimated that 7,800 nurses are working in the English-speaking countries of the Caribbean Community (CARICOM) (World Bank 2009). This works out at 1.25 nurses per 1,000 population, about one-tenth the concentration in some Organisation for Economic Co-operation and Development countries. This shortage has tangible impacts that could compromise the ability of CARICOM countries to meet their key health care service needs, especially in disease prevention and care. The shortage of highly trained nurses undermines the capacity of these countries to offer quality health care, precisely when they are striving to become more competitive and attract businesses and retirees as pillars of growth.

A lack of effective financing in the health sector adds to the health system's challenges. In 2007, government financed more than half of health care services in Eastern Caribbean countries, with general government expenditure on health as a percentage of total health expenditure ranging from 36.1 to 82.7 percent. Private expenditure on health is mostly out-of-pocket payments, ranging from 75.2 to 100 percent of total private expenditure, supplemented by a very small commercial insurance sector. Total health expenditure as a percentage of gross domestic product ranges from 4.9 to 8.5 percent (table 1.3). Poverty and unemployment rates

Table 1.3 Health Care Financing, Latest Available Year

Expenditure type	Antigua and Barbuda	Dominica	Grenada	St. Kitts and Nevis	St. Lucia	St. Vincent and the Grenadines
Total expenditure on health as a percentage of gross domestic product	4.9	6.0	6.3	6.4	8.5	5.2
External resources on health as a percentage of total expenditure on health	<0.5	1.5	<0.5	0.0	0.0	0.0
General government expenditure on health as a percentage of total expenditure on health	64.5	70.6	47.3	36.1	55.3	82.7
General government expenditure on health as a percentage of general government expenditure	14.7	11.6	9.6	7.3	15.0	14.7
Out-of-pocket expenditure as % of private expenditure on health	75.2	91.4	95.8	89.5	94.9	100.0
Total expenditure per capita on health at purchasing power parity (national currency units per US$)	1,020.9	596.8	728.8	1,332.3	897.6	554.5
General government expenditure per capita on health per capita at purchasing power parity (national currency units per US$)	658.2	421.3	345.0	481.4	496.3	458.5

Source: WHO, latest year available.

show that the two highest-income countries in the region (Antigua and Barbuda and St. Kitts and Nevis) have the lowest expenditure rates, and that the two lowest-income countries (Dominica and St. Vincent and the Grenadines) have the highest rates.

A lack of up-to-date, reliable health data and information hampers the ability of Eastern Caribbean countries to address their health sector challenges. Some progress is being made in this area, with a number of countries developing health information systems, establishing monitoring and evaluation plans to implement patient-monitoring and -tracking systems, and strengthening the capacity of monitoring and evaluation personnel to analyze and use data. Despite these efforts, management information systems remain fragmented and of questionable quality, and so are of limited use in informing policy decisions. Finally, the quality of the data still needs improving.

CARICOM Road Map to Strengthen the Health Workforce

In response to the change in demographics and its implication for health, CARICOM put in place the Road Map for Strengthening the Caribbean Health Workforce 2012–17—a strategy aimed at providing the region with a better-equipped and more effective health workforce in five years. The road map was developed with the support of Caribbean regional bodies and international cooperation, and under the leadership of the Pan American Health Organization. It addresses national policies and regional infrastructure, and its framework focuses on people-centered development, user involvement and participation, leadership in public health coordinated across the region, outcome-oriented planning and evaluation, and stable resourcing for health and social protection.

The road map sets 20 milestones along two broad themes: governance, and training and education. It also envisions securing better data and information; attaining greater policy development capacity; improving HRH planning capacity and strengthening management skills; establishing a more stable, transparent, and supportive work environment; improving quality and productivity; acquiring better skills to treat NCDs and meet primary health care needs; upgrading competencies for clinical staff; improving outcomes; and lowering costs.

Strengthening health systems and human resources is pivotal for addressing CARICOM's health and development issues, with a focus on primary health care, NCDs, family and child health, population aging, and mental health.

Many observers perceive weak governance as one of the greatest problems for strengthening HRH. Effective governance for this is the ability to enforce the rules and regulations that govern a health workforce; to provide leadership and oversight, and to competently allocate resources; and to manage performance and engage managers, providers, and stakeholders to improve the population's health.

The Nurse Workforce in the Eastern Caribbean • http://dx.doi.org/10.1596/978-1-4648-0830-2

Public and private sector regulation and quality assurance in particular need improving. For example, many Caribbean countries need to strengthen the steering role of their ministries of health in the strategic planning of the health workforce, and for monitoring, evaluation, and management. To this end, ministries of health must have skilled managers and decision makers who can evaluate evidence, formulate policies, plan strategically, and monitor trends and improvements if they are to effectively integrate the needs and multisector components of HRH planning and management. The migration of health professionals, particularly nurses, also needs to be addressed, because this is stretching the capacity of the health workforce and adds staffing challenges to HRH planners. Recruitment and retention policies and schemes need to be evaluated and implemented to mitigate pull factors, and improved working conditions are needed to mitigate push factors.

The evolving needs of the region's health systems need to be linked to training and education programs that address the competency requirements of health care providers. Equipping them with the necessary skills in long-term care, chronic disease management, and preventive care will help address the needs of aging populations. Better care can also lead to fewer incidences of NCDs, conditions that require a long-term care management approach. The changing epidemiological profile necessitates that providers rely on a more holistic approach to patient-centered care, one that addresses the lifestyle, culture, and behavior of patients. But many CARICOM countries lack in-country specialization training, and have to rely on the University of the West Indies' campuses in the region for specialized training.

References

World Bank. 2009. *The Nurse Labor and Education Market in the English-Speaking CARICOM: Issues and Options for Reform.* Washington, DC: World Bank.

———. 2011. "The Growing Burden of Non-Communicable Diseases in the Eastern Caribbean." Working Paper 67682, World Bank, Washington, DC. http://siteresources .worldbank.org/LACEXT/Resources/informe2no_jamaica.pdf.

CHAPTER 2

The Noncommunicable Disease Landscape in the Eastern Caribbean

Introduction

Noncommunicable diseases (NCDs) account for 70 percent of years of life lost because of premature mortality in the Eastern Caribbean, compared to a global average of 50 percent. NCDs also impose a heavy economic burden on patients, their families, and society. Data from Eastern Caribbean countries show the annual cost for treating a diabetic patient ranges from US$322 to US$769, and in St. Lucia caring for NCD patients represents 36 percent of total annual household expenditure for care (World Bank 2011). If Eastern Caribbean countries are to effectively address the NCD burden, they must be able to shift from providing episodic care based on prescribing medication to the comprehensive management of these diseases, which relies on more efficient approaches to improve the health outcomes of NCD patients. To this end, Eastern Caribbean countries have adopted a chronic care model (CCM) that pursues a more comprehensive, integrated care model to address NCDs, rather than focusing on individual diseases.

NCD Service Delivery

The Eastern Caribbean's CCM is an evidence-based, conceptual framework that sets out the changes in health care systems that are needed to help health care providers, particularly those working in primary care, and improve outcomes in patients suffering from chronic illness. The model fosters the development of informed and involved patients, as well as prepared and proactive health care teams, which can be more effective in treating chronic illness.

The CCM encompasses four components—self-management support, delivery system design, decision support, and clinical information systems. Self-management involves providing information and support to enable patients (and their families) to better care for their illness. Delivery system design focuses on the need to convert a traditional system for addressing acute illnesses into a more comprehensive system that introduces strategies to make the best use of resources. Some of these approaches may involve engaging nonphysician members of a practice team and providing them with clear, complementary roles; and making sure that nurse care managers and outreach workers are available to patients with more complex conditions or care needs so that health personnel can provide close follow-up and help increase adherence to treatment. The component for decision support emphasizes the need for health care providers to have access to the expertise necessary to care for patients, such as evidence-based practice guidelines and protocols that ensure provider teams know of effective treatments. The component for clinical information systems highlights the critical nature of these systems in providing timely and useful data about individual patients and populations of patients, regardless of whether the data come in electronic or hard-copy form (Epping-Jordan and others 2004).

In the Eastern Caribbean, the CCM is implemented across primary, secondary, and tertiary levels of care, targeting health centers and polyclinics at the primary health care level (table 2.1).

The responsibility for care rests on providers and patients. The functions and responsibilities outlined in the CCM include nursing care, prevention, health promotion, early detection and treatment, and rehabilitation. Health care staff are trained in the CCM through regional "training of trainers" sessions conducted by the Pan American Health Organization. As part of the CCM's implementation, countries strive to strengthen their chronic disease programs, improve access to technology and essential medicines, increase the competency of their health workforces, facilitate the reorientation of their health services, foster the

Table 2.1 Primary Health Care NCD Prevention and Treatment Services

Treatment services	Dominica	Grenada	St. Lucia	St. Vincent and the Grenadines
Population screening	X	X	X	X
Health promotion and education (clients and families)	X	X	X	X
Specialized medical clinics	X	X	X	X
Foot care services	X	X	X	X
Physical activity	X	X	X	X
Monthly clinics	X	X	X	X
Eye screening	X	X	X	X
Early detection for cancers	X	X	X	X
HBA1C testing	X	X	X	X
Cholesterol testing	X	X	X	X
Nutritional counseling	X	X	X	X
Workplace wellness programs	X	X	X	X
School screening	X	X	X	X

Source: Interviews with the ministries of health in each country during May and June 2015.
Note: NCD = noncommunicable disease.

development of evidence-based guidelines, facilitate the creation of health information systems, and develop self-management programs.

Despite the commitment of Eastern Caribbean countries to implement the CCM across the different levels of care, challenges remain. One is that they are unable to provide some types of care, which must be accessed in other countries. Dominica and St. Vincent and the Grenadines, for example, do not provide tertiary care, and although Grenada and St. Lucia have tertiary care, it is very limited and can be prohibitively expensive. The lack of a full range of in-country health services leads to gaps in the CCM's implementation across the different levels of care. Eastern Caribbean countries also face challenges in implementing aspects of the CCM, including the self-management component, which is critical for ensuring that patients take an active role to prevent and address NCDs. The difficulty here is that patients tend to rely on curative approaches to disease management, and that the self-management component requires that patients themselves change their behavior, and this takes time.

Implications of a Changing Burden of Disease

The rise in NCDs—and the attendant increased disease burden—has implications for how health workers should be regulated and incentivized, particularly nurses who are on the frontlines of care.

To maximize the acquisition of skills, staff training programs that focus on NCD care, management, and prevention should be introduced at the preservice level. Basic training in the management of chronic NCDs and the Pan American Health Organization's training of trainers for the CCM's implementation are offered in country. Although this training tries to reach all nurses, it is usually conducted after they have completed formal training and are already practicing. Significant advantages could be derived by specialized NCD training at the preservice level as part of the teaching curriculum. In this way, new generations of nurses would be well versed in delivering and monitoring the quality of NCD services by the time they complete their studies. Although this training is available, it has not resulted in enough nurses with specialized skills to address NCDs. For example, St. Lucia has only one nurse trained in diabetology and one nurse trained in oncology.[1] The number of nurses with specialized skills in such areas needs to be increased in all Eastern Caribbean countries to effectively address NCDs.

Amid the increasing burden of NCDs, nurses will play a greater and recognized role in strengthening the monitoring of these diseases. This should ensure that national-level data are captured, and support decision making on the delivery and management of services and resource allocation. It is generally understood that throughout the Eastern Caribbean, nurses are the ones who enter data into health information systems at the point-of-care level in health centers and facilities. And this is precisely why efforts to strengthen NCD data collection, monitoring, and input into health information systems should be directed and coordinated with and through nurses.

The nurse workforce needs to be motivated to take on the more complex tasks in NCD service delivery. To this end, regulations should be revised to create greater opportunities for career advancement across the different nursing cadres. This would provide nurses with a clear career path, from nursing assistants to community health nurses, nursing administrators, public health nurse supervisors, family nurse practitioners, psychiatric nurse practitioners, midwives, and registered nurses. Interviews conducted with nurses as part of this study revealed that they have an intrinsic motivation and natural commitment for entering the nurse workforce. However, they expressed concerns over the increased workload involved in properly providing NCD prevention and treatment services. This involves longer office hours for one-on-one counselling, increased patient follow-up to ensure adherence to treatment, increased administrative work to register NCD data in the proper forms, and more time spent conducting awareness sessions on healthy lifestyles to catchment populations in support of NCD prevention. Nurses are already taking on this extra work, but providing opportunities for career advancement could be an important incentive for encouraging them to perform their current duties well and could provide a way for them to comfortably suggest innovations for addressing NCD challenges.

Strategies to Address NCDs

Eastern Caribbean countries have embarked on various strategies to address NCDs. Two strategies shared by the four case study countries (Dominica, Grenada, St. Lucia, and St. Vincent and the Grenadines) involve task shifting—whereby tasks are delegated, where appropriate, to less specialized health workers—and implementing the so-called chronic care passport model. This is a patient card used by those with chronic conditions such as diabetes, hypertension, and chronic obstructive pulmonary disease. The chronic care passport model has direct technical assistance and support from the Pan American Health Organization.

Task shifting has empowered nurses to increasingly participate in data collection and monitoring of NCD patients, patient follow-up and adherence to treatment, and training on and awareness about healthy lifestyles in support of NCD prevention. Although this approach has clearly empowered nurses, it has also added to their workloads, especially because no clear understanding of task shifting has been implemented across other health workforce cadres. Going forward, the task-shifting approach could transition into a task-sharing approach whereby a team of health professionals provide patient-centered care by sharing—and not by delegating downward—tasks and responsibilities.

The second shared strategy, the chronic care passport model, was developed to strengthen primary health care and the integrated, population-based management of chronic diseases. Thus, it was designed for the first level of care, but it could be applied in other settings. In line with the CCM, the chronic care passport model acknowledges the central role of patients in managing their health through self-management programs supported by health policies and community organizations.

Note

1. Interview with the St. Lucia Ministry of Health's Health Planning Unit, June 2015.

References

Epping-Jordan, J. E., S. D. Pruitt, R. Bengoa, and E. H. Wagner. 2004. "Improving the Quality of Health Care for Chronic Conditions." *Quality and Safety in Health Care* 13 (4): 299–305. http://qualitysafety.bmj.com/content/13/4/299.full.pdf+html?sid=7d2efdca -40d7-47c5-a3c5-e426bc9bef8a.

World Bank. 2011. "The Growing Burden of Non-Communicable Diseases in the Eastern Caribbean." Working Paper 67682, World Bank, Washington, DC. http://siteresources .worldbank.org/LACEXT/Resources/informe2no_jamaica.pdf.

CHAPTER 3

Needs-Based Analysis of the Eastern Caribbean Nurse Workforce

Introduction

A literature review was used for a needs-based analysis of the human resources for health in Dominica, Grenada, St. Lucia, and St. Vincent and the Grenadines, the four case study countries. A needs-based approach estimates the number and type of health services required to be delivered based on the health needs of a given population. This estimate assumes that all health needs will be met and relies on technical expertise and judgments to provide guidance on what the most appropriate services are to meet those needs (Dreesch and others 2005). Even though this approach has some limitations, it can provide a snapshot comparison across countries of the capacity, in relation to numbers, of the health workforce.

Density Level

Dominica, Grenada, St. Lucia, and St. Vincent and the Grenadines have all achieved the minimum target for health worker density. According to recent Pan American Health Organization data, the overall density of doctors and nurses in these four countries is adequate in terms of the Caribbean baseline. But this has not consistently translated into the necessary density of primary health care skills (table 3.1).

Based on numbers alone, the four case study countries have enough trained nurses to provide adequate care for their populations. And, according to Pan American Health Organization guidelines, Dominica meets global benchmarks for the number of primary care nurses, although the country wants to hire more. Dominica had 419 nursing positions in 2014, of which 358 were filled (partly by nurses working in temporary slots); 293 of these nurses worked in primary care, and less than 1 percent were foreign.[1] St. Lucia also wants to increase its number of nurses: the country has approximately 500 nurses, 80–85 of whom are primary care nurses. Based on a needs assessment, St. Lucia requires an additional

Table 3.1 NDC Health Resources by Professional Category

Professional category	Dominica		Grenada		St. Lucia		St. Vincent and the Grenadines	
	Total (no.)	Per 10,000 population	Total (no.)	Per 10,000 population	Total (no.)	Per 10,000 population	Total (no.)	Per 10,000 population
Doctors	124	17.1	69	7.6	130	7.5	62	5.8
Nurses, midwives	370	50.9	398	43.9	329	19.0	268	25.2
Nurses, midwives, nursing assistants	562	77.3	NA	NA	371	21.4	208	19.6
Rehabilitation specialists	4	0.6	5	0.6	16	0.9	5	0.5
Nutritionists	1	0.1	1	0.1	7	0.4	8	0.8
Doctors, nurses, midwives	494	68.0	467	51.5	459	26.5	330	31.1
All health care providers	739	101.7	632	69.7	856	49.5	699	65.8
All health workers	824	113.4	974	107.3	1,485	85.8	923	86.9

Source: Figures drawn from information collected by the Pan American Health Organization from 2008 and 2012 as part of its Regional Goals for Human Resources in Health 2007–15 initiative.
Note: NA = not available; NCD = noncommunicable disease.

301 nurses to be able to deliver care in line with the country's strategic plan. Since 2007, St. Vincent and the Grenadines has increased the number of nurses it trains from 35 each year to 100, and the government sends excess trained nurses to other countries.

Even though the number of trained nurses in the Eastern Caribbean is sufficient, many of them are near retirement age—and this cohort includes the most skilled nurses. So even though enough new nurses are available to draw on, younger nurses coming into the workforce lack experience. The efforts of the four case study countries to hire additional nurses are hampered by budgetary constraints, such as the unofficial hiring freeze currently in place. To bridge the gap, they are relying on the temporary hiring of retired nurses. In St. Lucia, 80 percent of specialist nursing positions are filled by retired nurses.

Fiscal constraints are also hindering the ability to hire and absorb newly trained nurses to fill the slots of retired nurses. Grenada, for example, graduates more nurses than it is able to hire. Structural adjustments include a hiring freeze, which means no new positions can be created and existing positions must be left vacant. The Grenadian government has made arrangements for Trinidad and Tobago to hire many of its excess nurse capacity. However, given Trinidad and Tobago's better pay and benefits, this could eventually draw nurses, particularly midwives, away from Grenada, resulting in a shortage of trained nurses there.

Lack of Primary Health Care and Specialized Skills

Although Eastern Caribbean countries are meeting their overall health worker density targets, the availability of primary health care skills is less than optimal (table 3.2).

Table 3.2 Human Resources for Health Targets for Primary Health Care

Indicator	Target	Dominica	Grenada	St. Lucia	St. Vincent and the Grenadines
Human resources for health density (per 10,000 population)	25	Target achieved	53	41	25
Primary health care teams with broad range of skills (%)	NA	100	80	97	NA
Proportion of doctors in primary health care (%)	40	35	100	30	NA
Proportion of workers with public health skills (%)	70	70	1	83	NA
Proportion of managers with public health skills (%)	60	78	83	75	NA

Source: Figures drawn from information collected by the Pan American Health Organization from 2008 to 2012 as part of its Regional Goals for Human Resources in Health 2007–15 initiative.
Note: NA = not available.

Dominica is a particular concern: its demographic shifts are resulting in the emergence of large new communities, which are creating an imbalance in the demand and use of primary health care services. Indeed, Dominica may need to redraw its health districts—and shift resources accordingly—if it is to meet this challenge. The country may also need to increase the number of physicians in the primary health care system—and carefully consider the skill sets and competencies that they bring. Grenada is meeting targets for team competencies in primary health care and coverage of public health skills, but it is only just meeting them. Grenada also has enough primary care nurses, but absenteeism is a problem, leaving hospitals and clinics with insufficient coverage. St. Lucia has primary health care teams with broad skill sets, and is meeting targets for the proportions of workers and managers with public health skills. However, like Dominica, St. Lucia needs to increase the number of physicians in the public health care system, and carefully consider the skill sets and competencies that they bring. St. Vincent and the Grenadines has no available data on primary health care teams and public health skills.

Dominica is dealing with a shortage of specialist nurses and medical officers in gynecology, general surgery, pathology, anesthesiology, cardiology, intensive care nursing, operating and surgery, ophthalmology, and pediatric nursing. The country has only one neonatal nurse and not enough midwives, a shortage partly caused by the requirement that before being trained as midwives, nurses must first be licensed as registered nurses. Grenada also has a shortage of nurses with specializations, including training in dialysis, oncology, psychiatry, family practice, intensive care, geriatrics, and community health. St. Lucia also lacks nurse specialists, particularly those trained in intensive care, oncology, nephrology, pediatrics, and neonatal care, as does Dominica, which is also experiencing a shortage of midwives. St. Vincent and the Grenadines is facing shortages in family nurses, nurse practitioners, and nurses trained in diabetes and emergency care.

Because noncommunicable diseases have steadily increased, the gap between available specialized skills and the limited training opportunities has become more critical, causing East Caribbean countries to rely on nurses from abroad. As of writing, the staffing profile in Dominica, Grenada, St. Lucia, and St. Vincent and the Grenadines does not meet the requirements indicated by their current or projected noncommunicable disease profile.

Throughout the Caribbean, the prevalence of diabetes has led to an increase in amputations. But St. Vincent and the Grenadines has no nurses trained in rehabilitating amputees. Because specialty training is not offered in country, nurses have to get the necessary training elsewhere. However, with limited career advancement opportunities in the clinic setting, no direct incentives exist for obtaining specialist training. This is a disincentive for nurses to pursue specialist training, and is happening amid a shortage of specialized nurses and the need for training opportunities. Consequently, better-qualified nurses and specialists are being recruited by other countries that pay better. To address both problems, health personnel from other countries including the Philippines are being recruited. Dominica, for example, hires specialist nurses and doctors from China, and doctors, specialist nurses, and intensive care nurses from Cuba.

A needs-based approach provides an overview of the capacity of the health workforce based on estimates and population needs, but it has limitations. For example, estimates of needs include only a limited category of health workers in an analysis of human resources for health when, in fact, most health care delivery systems rely on a much broader category of health workers. Moreover, a needs-based approach does not consider the different perceptions of patient and client needs as viewed by various health workers, who may hold vastly different perceptions based on their belief systems and professional judgments. The figures collected from a needs-based approach can be used as an indicator of global trends, but not as actual benchmarks against which the number of needed health workers for country-level planning purposes can be calculated.

Note

1. The slight discrepancy between the figures provided by Dominica's Ministry of Health in March 2014 and the Pan American Health Organization's figures included in table 3.1 is because of staff fluctuations at two different points in time.

Reference

Dreesch, N., C. Dolea, M. R. Dal Poz, A. Goubarev, O. Adams, and others. 2005. "An Approach to Estimating Human Resource Requirements to Achieve the Millennium Development Goals: Health Policy Plan." *Health Policy and Planning* 20 (5): 267–76. doi:10.1093/heapol/czi036.

Assessing the Eastern Caribbean Nurse Workforce Using a Health Labor Market Approach

Introduction

The supply and demand of health care workers are the two independent economic forces that make up the health labor market (Scheffler 2008). The interplay of these forces determines wages and other forms of compensation (such as benefits and housing allowances), the number of health workers employed, and the hours they work. How these two forces come together also determines the geographic distribution of health workers and where they work, such as in a hospital or a clinic.

As well as supply and demand, a more comprehensive picture of the health labor market should include the productivity and performance of health workers. Productivity is measured as patient visits per hour, and performance is based on whether health care workers do what they were trained to do (Scheffler 2012). A health labor market analysis for the Eastern Caribbean would not be complete without an assessment of the global health labor market, given the regional initiatives channeled through the Caribbean Community and the Organisation of Eastern Caribbean States, which govern human resources for health in these countries.

Supply of Nurses

This study assesses the supply of nurses for the Eastern Caribbean nurse workforce through a review of several interrelated aspects, including the cost of training, number of vacancies, types of training offered, number of graduates, wages, migration, death and retirement in the profession, and personal preferences.

The cost of training nurses in the four case study countries (Dominica, Grenada, St. Lucia, and St. Vincent and the Grenadines) involves out-of-pocket expenses for student nurses, though scholarships are offered for specific levels of training. The European Union, for example, finances such scholarship programs. In St. Lucia, these scholarships support students training in midwifery, family nursing, and psychiatric nursing. In the second year of this program, 14 midwives, two family nurses, and one psychiatric nurse were trained.

Because in-country training is so limited, those seeking advanced or specialized training go abroad. In all four case study countries, in-country training includes a three-year associate degree or diploma course in general nursing, and an additional one and a half years of training for midwifery. Further training can be obtained at the University of the West Indies in Jamaica, which offers a two-year master's degree in family and psychiatric nursing. Nurses throughout the Caribbean also go to Cuba for further training, and some 124 general nurses from St. Lucia have been trained there. For-profit foreign training institutions in the region, such as Ross University School of Medicine in Dominica, Monroe College in St. Lucia (both U.S. colleges), and St. George's University in Grenada, offer training in public health and other health areas, but these institutions tend to cater to international rather than local students.

The categories of nurses in the four case study countries are registered nurses, midwives, psychiatric nurses, family nurses, public health nurse supervisors, nursing administrators, community health nurses, and nursing assistants. Nursing vacancies are few in all four countries, and those that do open up are limited to specialized categories, such as psychiatric and family nurses, and midwives.

It is unclear whether migration and retirement translates into vacancies. Although posts are created according to a country's needs, the decision on whether to fill them rests with the ministry of public service, and is outside the control of the ministry of health. To create a post, the nursing administrator or hospital department head makes a recommendation to the ministry of health's permanent secretary, who authorizes the post and provides the rationale for its creation to the ministry of public service. The ministry then sends a request to the ministry of finance to determine whether funds are available to cover the post. All four case study countries face the situation that retiring nurses will not necessarily be replaced. Retired nurses with specialized skills often reenter the nurse labor market. Just over half of St. Lucia's retired nurses take jobs as midwives.

Even though the salary structure for nurses reflects career progression, openings for career advancement are limited. Salaries are determined by a fixed structure set by the government, and salaries increase as skills and certifications are acquired (table 4.1 shows the salary progression by nursing categories and grade levels in St. Lucia). However, the opportunity to acquire more responsibilities and better remuneration is limited, because fewer positions open up at the higher levels. That said, nurses and officials interviewed for this study emphasized that the motivation for entering the nurse workforce was

Table 4.1 Monthly Nurses Pay, by Category, in St. Lucia, 2015

Category	Grade	Salary (EC$)
Registered nurses	9	3,505
Registered nurses	10	3,820
Registered nurses	11	4,167
Community health nurses	12	4,513
Public health nursing supervisors	13	4,860
Nurse leaders	14	5,159
Nurse leaders	15	5,482
Nurse leaders	18	6,467

Source: Ministry of Health.

vocational rather than financial. And while they acknowledged that limitations on career and salary advancement can be a disincentive, other factors determined why they stayed in the profession.

Demand for Nurses

The demand for nurses in the Eastern Caribbean—as is the case with their supply—is assessed through various factors related to training, cost, wages, and regulation. Within these factors lie key aspects such as the number of applicants, cost of tuition, expected wages and wages offered, demand for health care, and the overall regulation of the policies governing the nurse workforce (Carpio and Santiago Bench 2015).

For training and cost, no recruitment strategy to enroll students into nursing programs is in place in any of the four case study countries. Even so, nursing programs seem to be adequately staffed, going by local information and this study's analysis of the opportunities for entering the nurse workforce. Students enrolled in nursing programs expressed an interest in pursuing specialized training, but high tuition costs and leaving home to study abroad were seen as disincentives.

On wages, as noted earlier, salary is not the main motivation for becoming a nurse. Salary scales in all the case study countries are well known to anyone considering a nursing career since they are determined by ministries of public service. And those entering nurse training programs are generally aware of the limitations on advancing up the salary scale given the very few vacancies that open up in the higher salary grades and more specialized nursing categories.

Regulations governing the nurse labor market play an important role in the demand for nurses. As discussed earlier, this is high on the frontlines of service delivery for noncommunicable diseases, and this pressure led to the regulation on task shifting at the level of health provision outlining the clinical and nonclinical tasks that could be taken on. Other regulations affecting the demand for nurses include rules related to creating and filling posts and the setting of salaries. Because these decisions lie outside ministries of health, their ability to make decisions that support the demands and needs of the nurse labor market is limited.

Productivity of the Nurse Workforce

This study collected information on dual practice, deployment of the health workforce, and absenteeism to help to assess the productivity of the nurse workforce in the Eastern Caribbean. In dual practice, health workers employed in government facilities also work in the private sector, either in individual practice or in clinics or hospitals (Akiko and others 2014). Deployment of the health workforce entails management decisions that assign health workers to their posts. The deployment pattern for nurses is determined by numerous factors, including balancing the geographic availability of nurses and ensuring that technical needs such as disease outbreaks and specific health conditions are covered (Kazanjian, Pulcins, and Kerluke 1990). Absenteeism can be planned or unplanned: in the first case, the employer is aware that the employee will not be coming to work and can plan accordingly; in the second case, an employee simply fails to show up at work without giving the employer prior notice. This study focuses on unplanned absences (Belita, Mbindyo, and English 2013).

Dual practice is commonplace in the four case study countries. Nurses working in the public sector are required to get permission to work in the private sector, but, in practice, this does not happen, and so dual practice cannot be accurately tracked.

On deployment, nurses in all four countries are assigned according to the needs of the population and their qualifications. Deployment decisions are not guided by a clear urban-rural divide because these countries are small geographically and population-wise. Nurses are deployed near where they live to reduce travel time and to have them working in communities they know, with the rationale that this increases their efficiency.

Absenteeism is a problem in all four countries. Contributing factors include job dissatisfaction, overwork, and burnout, as found in a cross-sectional study on absenteeism in nursing conducted at Kingston Hospital in Jamaica (Carpio and Santiago Bench 2015). Despite an overall sense that absenteeism hinders performance, the four countries have not instituted key performance indicators to measure the impact of absenteeism on health service delivery or the quality of care.

Performance of the Nurse Workforce

This section looks at whether nurses are fulfilling the tasks that they have been trained for. Sanctions and rewards and incentives are among the mechanisms that have a direct impact on performance. The ministry of public service is responsible for sanctioning or promoting staff in all four case study countries. Their nursing councils, which have a role in hiring nurses, have some sanctioning powers, but none for rewards. Beyond these formal channels, some practices in clinics that come under the management of the ministry of health involve rewards and incentives. For example, the ministry of health finances the participation of nurses in local and overseas training to hone their skills. Straight monetary incentives are not offered in any of the four countries, but other incentives such as scholarships for further study and allowances for travel, uniforms, and laundry are used. Nurses are also given free health care as part of their package of benefits.

Any analysis of the health labor market in Eastern Caribbean countries must consider employment demands from and the attractions of the global health market. Nursing graduates in the Eastern Caribbean can sit the National Council Licensure Examination in their home countries to obtain nursing licenses for Canada and the United States. Both countries have made commitments to support the institutional strengthening of nurse training programs in the Eastern Caribbean, provide exchange opportunities for nurses from both regions, and support the training of tutors and instructors from the Eastern Caribbean in their home countries.

With regard to agreements that have international or regional scope in the global health labor market, all four case study countries are signatories to the General Agreement on Trade in Services, the Caribbean Community Single Market Economy, the World Health Organization's Global Code of Practice, and the Pan American Health Organization's Regional Plan for Action for Human Resources for Health 2007–15. Dominica, Grenada, and St. Lucia are signatories to the International Labour Organization's Convention No. 97, which provides migrants with treatment no less favorable than that given to nationals. The General Agreement on Trade in Services and the Caribbean Community Single Market Economy, in particular, govern the free movement of services and, through the latter, the mutual recognition of diplomas and certificates across signatory countries. The World Health Organization's Code of Practice calls for upholding the principles of fairness and mutual benefit in the recruitment of health workers, and for plans and policies to be put in place for strengthening the health workforce, for developing institutional capacities, and for signatories to monitor the health workforce and evaluate policies. The four case study countries have developed human resources for health plans, and all allow their nurses to work in each other's countries. The Pan American Health Organization's regional action plan highlights the importance of developing national action plans for human resources for health, ensuring that the health workforce is appropriately deployed, and that mechanisms exist for cooperation. Eastern Caribbean countries have made advances in these areas (Kurowski and others 2012).

As well as having action plans for human resources for health (as outlined in table 3.2), these countries have made headway in the deployment of health workers with primary health care skills. Cooperation agreements for the supply of nurses to address shortages exist between Cuba and Dominica, Grenada, St. Lucia, and, until recently, St. Vincent and the Grenadines.

References

Akiko, M., E. Araujo, C. Cashin, J. Harris, N. Ikegami, and M. R. Reich. 2014. *Universal Health Coverage for Inclusive and Sustainable Development: A Synthesis of 11 Country Case Studies*. Directions in Development Series. Washington, DC: World Bank. doi:10.1596 /978-1-4648-0297-3.

Belita, A., P. Mbindyo, and M. English. 2013. "Absenteeism amongst Health Workers: Developing a Typology to Support Empiric Work in Low-Income Countries and Characterizing Reported Associations." *Human Resources for Health* 11: 34. http://www.human-resources-health.com/content/11/1/34.

Carpio, C., and N. Santiago Bench. 2015. *The Health Workforce in Latin America and the Caribbean: An Analysis of Colombia, Costa Rica, Jamaica, Panama, Peru, and Uruguay*. Directions in Development Series. Washington, DC: World Bank. doi:10.1596/978-1-4648-0594-3.

Kazanjian, A., I. R. Pulcins, and K. Kerluke. 1990. *Nurse Deployment Patterns: Examples for Health Human Resources Management*. University of British Columbia, Division of Health Services Research and Development, Health Manpower Research Unit. doi:10.14288/1.0075923.

Kurowski, C., C. Carpio, M. Vujicic, L. O. Gostin, and T. Baytor. 2012. "Towards a Regional Strategy to Strengthen the Nurse Workforce of the English-Speaking CARICOM: International Legal Instruments, Agreements, and Obligations." Health, Nutrition, and Population Discussion Paper 69374, World Bank, Washington, DC.

Scheffler, R. M. 2008. *Is There a Doctor in the House? Market Signals and Tomorrow's Supply of Doctors*. Stanford, CA: Stanford University Press.

———. 2012. *The Labour Market for Human Resources for Health in Low- and Middle-Income Countries*. Geneva: World Health Organization.

CHAPTER 5

Nursing Education and Training in the Eastern Caribbean

Introduction

Based on recent baseline data collection, Eastern Caribbean countries have an adequate supply of human resources for health (HRH), which meet or exceed the World Health Organization's recommended minimum of 25 HRH personnel per 10,000 population. The big question, however, is whether the adequate supply of HRH is sufficiently trained in competencies for managing noncommunicable diseases (NCDs). If NCDs are to be prevented or effectively managed, strategies for combatting these diseases should incorporate an HRH component to facilitate the planning and management of the health workforce responsible for NCD treatment and prevention.

Most Eastern Caribbean countries have a public technical or community college offering associate degrees and, in some cases, bachelor of science degrees. But students seeking further education or specialization must look to universities abroad, but this is expensive and only a few scholarships are offered to foreign students.

The University of the West Indies is the main source of postgraduate training for NCDs. Across its four campuses in Barbados, Jamaica, and Trinidad and Tobago, 63 courses were offered in 23 subjects that deal with primary or tertiary health care and NCDs in the 2013/14 academic year. The University of the West Indies in Jamaica offers training for family nurses, and Barbados Community College offers training in community health nursing, administration, and nurse education. Laboratory training is available in Jamaica, Trinidad and Tobago, and the United States. But very few of the region's universities offer a comprehensive postgraduate program for HRH.

Planned learning, training, and development activities are the tools that organizations use to improve employee skills and knowledge. In the health sector, training is the key to improving the performance of both individual health workers and the sector as a whole. Training can involve various approaches, such as structured courses, mentoring, coaching, job shadowing, peer exchange, and self-learning. Competency-based training is a useful alternative to time-based models for in-service and continuing professional development training of HRH. Competency-based training allows the health sector to identify training needs based on service delivery requirements.

The Pan American Health Organization (PAHO) offers several short-term training opportunities for health personnel in the Eastern Caribbean, and works closely with ministries of health to design training modalities based on needs identified by the ministries. This training covers, among other things, management and technical clinical skills. Nongovernmental organizations also provide targeted training in some Eastern Caribbean countries. The following sections look the education and training of nurses in the four case study countries (Dominica, Grenada, St. Lucia, and St. Vincent and the Grenadines).

Dominica

Dominica has one public nursing school, the Faculty of Nursing at Dominica State College. Its nursing programs include the following:

- *Certificate in Practical Nursing.* A one-and-a-half-year program in which nursing graduates are trained as nursing assistants. They are not permitted to administer medication.
- *Primary Care Nursing Program.* This includes practical nursing and midwifery training. Graduates provide supplementary care to doctors.
- *General Nursing Program.* A two-and-a half-year program to train registered nurses.
- *Post-Registered Nurse Midwifery Program.* For general nurses who have handled 25 successful deliveries under supervision. This requirement limits the number of nurses eligible to apply; 15 students a year are accepted into the program.
- *Bachelor of science in nursing.* The program, begun in September 2014, includes additional courses and clinical rotations. The program was introduced after the Regional Nursing Body lobbied for a bachelor of science nursing program, and in response to a government decision to have all entry-level nurses hold at least a bachelor's degree by 2011. Entry into the program is competitive: as of March 2014, 60 applications were submitted for 20–40 positions. The college's ability to accept more students is limited by lack of clinical space, supervision, and faculty numbers. Access to the heavily government-subsidized program is by no means restrictive: costs are quite low—EC$50 per credit, and students who cannot afford this are offered loans—and entry requirements easy. Some government scholarships are available. To be accepted into the program, applicants must pass five key subjects in grades 1 and 2, including English, math, and science. Students are then required to take a one-year, pre-health program and pass it with a grade point average of at least 2.5. Those interviewed over the program had positive responses. The Regional Nursing Body sets the curriculum and the qualifying exams, thus ensuring consistency

in training throughout the region. The college works closely with the Ministry of Health to design courses that meet the needs of the population. Its pass rate was 90 percent at the time of writing.[1]

As well as the public nursing program, two private universities offer training: Ross University School of Medicine, which graduates physicians, and All Saints University, which offers a premedical program.

Apart from midwifery, Dominica offers no specialty certification opportunities. Higher-level nursing training and specialization outside the country are available in Barbados (Community Health College, offering training in community health nursing, administration, and nursing education) and Jamaica (University of the West Indies, offering training for family nurses).

PAHO and several nongovernmental organizations provide short-term training for health workers. PAHO and Ministry of Health training includes workshops on management, communication, and technology. This helps fill gaps in competencies, but is no substitute for the extensive specialty training that is needed. In the past, PAHO provided significant support for training, but this was hit by budgetary constraints. PAHO also provides fellowships for students seeking advanced training outside their home countries, but this ended in 2014 because of budgetary constraints and management issues. Because participation in this training was not tracked, the same people often attended the workshops. And with no dissemination plan, knowledge was not passed on to other health care workers—a concern since many experienced nurses are near retirement.

Grenada

Grenada formerly had two nursing schools: one at T. A. Marryshow Community College (TAMCC) and one at St. George's University. The TAMCC program was moved to St. George's University in 2015. George's University offers a master's in public health and a master's in health management. The university is in discussions to merge its bachelor of sciences in nursing program with that of TAMCC. Midwifery is St. George's University's only specialization training for nursing.

As in all countries in the region, Grenada's curriculum and exams are standardized and set by the Regional Nursing Body.

Specialized training other than midwifery is not offered locally. Some medical professionals travel to China for specialized training, which is free to Grenadians, or to neighboring countries for training, including the four campuses of the University of the West Indies.

As well as the formal nursing program, the Caribbean Public Health Agency, the Joint United Nations Programme on HIV/AIDS, PAHO, and the U.S. President's Emergency Plan for AIDS Relief offer short-term nursing training courses and workshops focusing key needs identified by the Ministry of Health, including customer relations, foot care, eye screening, primary health care development, dialysis, infection control, and mental health. The ministry has relied heavily on PAHO for short-term training, but workshops and scholarships were cut back in recent years because of budgetary constraints.

Training is needed in management, customer service, human resources, and monitoring and evaluation to improve the quality of nursing in Grenada. Currently, no management training specific to nursing is offered. The main option for this is an online program at the University of the West Indies in Jamaica and Barbados, or a two-year program in Trinidad and Tobago. However, neither of these programs is government funded, so cost is a barrier for many. Training in customer service, both in the nursing school curriculum and after graduation as part of ongoing training, is needed to improve patient care. Training in human resources would help provide needed skills within the Ministry of Health to improve its management of the health workforce. Monitoring and evaluation is an important component of health care planning and is needed at all levels of health management in Grenada.

St. Lucia

St. Lucia has one public nursing school (Saint Lucia Community College) and three offshore universities (Spartan Health Science University, American International Medical University, St. Helen University). The three offshore universities were initially created to train locals for international nursing jobs, but they also train nurses to work in St. Lucia. Programs offered include a two-year associate degree in general nursing and the option to do an online bachelor of sciences in nursing through one of the off shore universities.

The needs of St. Lucia's health system and its health-related academic programs are not properly linked, and no clear system is in place to identify the gaps and needs in the health system and to ensure that they are covered in the nursing curriculum. Further, the nursing school does not have enough lecturers, which limits the number of courses.

The only specialist training is for midwifery, offered at the nursing school. Other specialist training is only available abroad, primarily at the University of the West Indies' campuses in Barbados, Jamaica, and Trinidad and Tobago.

Nurses working for five years are granted study leave. For those taking a bachelor's or master's degree, 100 percent of salary is provided for the first year of study, and 75 percent for the second. The government also offers a partial tuition refund for those who pass courses taken on study leave and agree to work in the public sector.

The main barrier to becoming a nurse in St. Lucia is financial. Students are required to either pay for nursing school upfront or take out loans. Graduating from secondary school and passing in five main subjects are prerequisites for studying nursing.

As well as traditional nursing education programs, St. Lucia offers significant short-term training, with PAHO, UNICEF (the United Nations Children's Fund), and nongovernmental organizations offering training focused on developing competencies.

St. Vincent and the Grenadines

The country has one nursing school, the St. Vincent and the Grenadines School of Nursing. Until recently, it had only a general nursing program, but the school now offers a bachelor of science in nursing. Its only specialization, however, is midwifery. For other specialized training, the country's nurses generally travel to the University of the West Indies' campuses, and some travel to Cuba. The government provides 100 percent of salary for the first year of study and 50 percent for the second, and graduates of specialized training move to a higher pay grade. Along with other countries in the region, high cost is the main barrier to studying nursing in St. Vincent and the Grenadines. And for those living in the Grenadines, travel costs are an additional barrier.

PAHO works with the Ministry of Health to identify health needs and priorities, and offers short-term training courses based on those needs, including health system development, environmental health, communicable and non-communicable diseases, and family and community health.

Note

1. Interview with Lilia Casey, dean of the Faculty of Health Sciences, Dominica State College.

CHAPTER 6

Legislation Supporting Human Resources for Health Planning and Management in the Eastern Caribbean

Introduction

An extensive review of the literature on generic human resources management practices and management practices specific to human resources for health (HRH) was conducted in August 2013 as part of this study.

Inventory of HRH-Related Legislation

The review helped in the preparation of an inventory of necessary legislation for effective HRH planning and management. This, in turn, became the basis for a checklist of four key pieces of legislation or statutes that a country should have in place to support HRH planning and management (table 6.1).

All four case study countries (Dominica, Grenada, St. Lucia, and St. Vincent and the Grenadines) have in place at least one of the four key pieces of legislation or statutes shown in table 6.1 to support HRH planning and management. Dominica and St. Lucia have enacted legislation covering essential services: the Essential Services Act and the Labour Act of 2006, section VIII (2) in Dominica, and the Regulation of Disputes in the Essential Services in St. Lucia.

All four countries have enacted legislation covering trade union formation and industrial relations: the Trade Union Act and the Industrial Relations Act in Dominica; the Labour Relations Act of 1999 (amended 2000 and 2003) in Grenada; the Labour Act of 2006, sections VII (trade union formation and operation) and VIII (industrial relations and disputes) in St. Lucia; and the Trade Unions Act of 1950 (amended 1988), the Trade Disputes (Arbitration and Inquiry) Act of 1940 (amended 1987), and the trade union rules of 1990 in St. Vincent and the Grenadines.

Only St. Lucia among the four countries has legislation covering occupational health and safety in its Labour Act of 2006, section IV. All four have legislation covering the registration of health professionals, though there are differences in which types of practitioners are covered. For example, Dominica's Medical Act covers doctors and dentists as well as pharmacists and opticians, as does similar legislation in St. Lucia and St. Vincent and the Grenadines. Overall, the registration of the main HRH cadres in the case study countries are covered through these key acts.

All four case study countries have additional legislation to support HRH planning and management (table 6.2). Dominica, St. Lucia, and St. Vincent and the Grenadines have mental health acts, which highlight the importance that these countries attach to this critical issue. For nursing, St. Lucia's Family Nurse Practitioners Act of 1993 authorizes family nurse practitioners to prescribe certain drugs, which is vital to addressing noncommunicable diseases. Because of limited HRH on the frontlines, nurses can prescribe essential medications for treating these diseases. Additional HRH legislation in St. Lucia covers, among other areas, labor relations, environmental health, and the role of the Ministry of Health and its core function.

Table 6.1 Key Legislation for HRH Planning and Management

Legislation or statute	Dominica	Grenada	St. Lucia	St. Vincent and the Grenadines
Legislation covering essential services	Yes	No	Yes	No
Legislation covering trade unionizing and industrial relations; for example, labor code, trade union act, industrial relations act.	Yes	Yes	Yes	Yes
Legislation covering health and safety	No	No	Yes	No
Legislation covering registration of health professionals	Yes	Yes	Yes	Yes

Source: Desk review and field interviews conducted in March 2014.
Note: HRH = human resources for health.

Table 6.2 Additional Legislation for HRH Planning and Management

Dominica	Grenada
Labour Standards Act	Grenada Constitution Act (1973)
Mental Health Act	Employment Act (1999, amended 2000)
Public Service Act	Terms and Conditions of Employment Act (1968, amended 1990)
Environmental Health Services Act	Labour Relations Act (1999, amended 2000, 2003)
General Orders and Public Service Commission Regulations	National Insurance Act (1983, latest amendment 2011)
Hospitals and Health Care Facilities Act (2002)	Foreign Nationals and Commonwealth Citizens (Employment) Act (1968, amended 1972, 1978, 2001)
Roseau Hospital Ordinance Act	Caribbean Community Skilled Nationals Act (1995, amended 2006)
Accreditation Act	Public Health Act (1973, 1981)
Roseau Hospital Rules	Recruiting of Workers Act (1939)

table continues next page

Table 6.2 Additional Legislation for HRH Planning and Management *(continued)*

St. Lucia	*St. Vincent and the Grenadines*
Public Health Act (1971, revised 2001): covers health care services, occupational health and safety, veterinary services, and health risk factors; establishes the role of the Ministry of Health and its core function.	Public Health Act (1977): grants Ministry of Health broad authority to regulate and enforce health codes in private businesses and homes, including food production and storage, water purification, and mosquito control.
Mental Health Act (1957)	General Nursing Council Rules (1990): rules for health professionals provide for councils to oversee the registration and practice of medicine, nursing, and pharmacy.
The Hospital Ordinance (1992): covers charges and fees for hospital services and establishes responsibility for payment.	Milton Cato Memorial Hospital Schedule of Fees (1995)
Family Nurse Practitioners Act (1993): authorizes family nurse practitioners to prescribe certain drugs.	Mental Health Act (1958, amended 1991): regulates the conditions under which patients may be voluntarily admitted to the Mental Health Rehabilitation Center.

Source: Desk review and field interviews conducted in March 2014.
Note: HRH = human resources for health.

CHAPTER 7

Human Resources for Health Planning to Address Noncommunicable Diseases in the Eastern Caribbean

Introduction

A broad-based decrease in mortality, accompanied by rising morbidity associated with a growing prevalence of noncommunicable diseases (NCDs), is putting already stretched health resources under added pressure. Consequently, health services need to be bolstered by increasing their efficiency and quality of care, thus enabling limited resources to be used more effectively. Regardless of the specific epidemiological challenge, an important aspect of any health solution will always involve the human resources for health (HRH) sector. To address national health challenges, it is necessary to undertake evidence-based, strategic planning and policy development. This should consider government and ministry of health goals, epidemiological profile, workforce characteristics, and workforce planning.

Role of HRH Planning in Combatting NCDs

To effectively combat the NCD epidemic, it is vital that monitoring, prevention, and management are part of comprehensive NCD programs, especially HRH strategic planning and development processes, which need to be considered at the institutional and ministry levels. Once included as part of a ministry of health strategy, it is paramount that both the infrastructure and HRH are in place to support strategic policies.

Although none of the four case study countries (Dominica, Grenada, St. Lucia, and St. Vincent and the Grenadines) have a formal HRH plan in place, they are trying to move toward that goal. Dominica has been discussing the development of an HRH policy for many years, and senior Ministry of Health officials want to develop a policy that aligns with the ministry's strategic plan.[1] But the effort has lacked a champion to make this a priority, and budgetary, personnel, and expertise constraints have stalled the process. St. Lucia hired a consultant in early 2014 to develop an HRH plan to address succession, retention, learning and development, performance, and leadership in alignment with the National Strategic Plan, which supports the delivery of primary health care. The plan envisages covering the private sector and data sharing of private sector health professionals to help fill gaps in the provision of specialized health services by allowing the Ministry of Health to engage private sector specialists when needed. However, the plan has no funding, so its development must wait for new staff or a human resources director to come on board. In St. Vincent and the Grenadines, Ministry of Health officials recognize the need to set up a human resources unit within the ministry, and to improve the management and planning for human resources. Before an HRH policy can be developed, however, the ministry needs to examine the country's epidemiological profile and complete the health sector's strategic plan to establish its priority areas, and then make HRH staffing decisions based on that.

Core HRH Planning Functions

Even with no specific HRH policies in place, Eastern Caribbean countries can still plan for HRH by assessing their progress in establishing four core HRH components—a national health plan, an HRH information system, an HRH management unit, and an HRH multisectoral taskforce (table 7.1).[2]

All four case study countries recognize the importance of having a national health plan, and either have one in place (Dominica and St. Lucia) or are developing one (Grenada and St. Vincent and the Grenadines). Dominica's public health sector is guided by the National Strategic Plan for Health 2012–19, comprising a health situational analysis, which provides the population's health profile, and an action plan, which identifies needs and priorities in health interventions. St. Lucia is updating its National Strategic Plan 2006–11, and Grenada and St. Vincent and the Grenadines are working with the Pan American Health Organization to develop strategic plans for health.

Table 7.1 Progress toward Establishing Core Components of HRH Planning

Core HRH planning component	Dominica	Grenada	St. Lucia	St. Vincent and the Grenadines
National plan for health	Yes	In progress	Yes	In progress
HRH information system	In progress	No	Yes	In progress
HRH management unit	No	No	In progress	No
HRH multisectoral taskforce	No	In progress	Yes	No

Source: Desk review and field interviews conducted in March 2014.
Note: HRH = human resources for health.

Although three of the four countries do not have health information systems in place, each has a central planning unit that to some degree collects HRH data. In Dominica, this is collected by the Establishment, Personnel, and Training Department, and includes biographic information on public sector employees and their skills and competencies. Grenada does not have an electronic health information system, and personnel records are kept as paper files. Because these files do not always record updates on education and training, it is not possible to search them for personnel that have undergone specific training or have specialized skills. St. Lucia's Corporate Planning Unit has a comprehensive database covering all HRH in the public and private health sectors, but the Ministry of Health does not have direct access to it (though it can request information from the unit). Within the ministry, the only data tracked are staff movements, such as vacation and retirement. In St. Vincent and the Grenadines, human resources data are managed in alignment with other ministries and, as in St. Lucia, the information tracked by the Ministry of Health is limited to staff movements. Dominica, Grenada, and St. Vincent and the Grenadines plan to enhance their HRH information systems by increasing their use of SmartStream payroll software to manage finances, human resources, assets, and performance management. Dominica also has a standalone, desktop human resources database, but it is not clear how it interacts with SmartStream. St. Lucia plans to develop a database for tracking health personnel information.

None of the four case study countries has an HRH management unit, and this limits human resource actions and decisions by ministries of health to purely administrative matters, such as vacation requests. No HRH department within these ministries is equipped to address more strategic human resources issues such as recruitment, retention, and the training necessary to meet health needs. And because of the centralized structure of these countries, all hiring and firing decisions are made by separate public service bodies. Some ministries of health may be involved in interviewing applicants and submitting hiring requests, but this is not the uniform practice. As a result, those interviewing prospective employees often do not have the technical knowledge to ascertain the quality of candidates. In short, keeping the human resources function outside ministries of health is hindering the strategic planning and management of health care personnel.

Of the four case study countries, only St. Lucia has set up a multisector taskforce, the National Human Resources Advisory Group, to address HRH issues. The taskforce, started in early 2014, was set up to bring together relevant stakeholders and pave the way for establishing partnerships between the public and private sectors to meet the country's HRH needs. It includes representatives from the Ministry of Finance, the Ministry of Public Services, the Ministry of Education, and the Ministry of Health (including nurses and doctors), as well as councils overseeing specific health sector areas and St. Jude and St. Victoria hospitals. As of writing, Grenada's attempts to establish a multisector HRH taskforce have stalled, and neither Dominica nor St. Vincent and the Grenadines has a taskforce.

Table 7.2 Progress in Enhanced HRH Planning

Enhanced HRH planning function	Dominica	Grenada	St. Lucia	St. Vincent and the Grenadines
HRH plan	No	No	In progress	No
HRH leadership	Yes	No	Yes	No
HRH champion in the Ministry of Health	No	No	Yes	No
Process for aligning HRH planning to Ministry of Health needs	No	No	Yes	No
HRH development and training plan	No	No	No	No
Process for evidence-based workforce planning	—	—	—	—
Process for aligning training needs to Ministry of Health requirements	No	No	No	No
Human resources policies and procedures	In progress	In progress	In progress	No
Financial and service delivery plan that balances reasonably expected health care resources and commitments	No	—	No	No
Conduct of national health accounts estimation	No	No	No	No
Mechanism for coordinating activities between the private and public health sectors	No	No	No	No
Mechanism for coordinating activities between community organizations and the public health sector	No	No	In progress	No

Source: Desk review and field interviews conducted in March 2014.
Note: — = not available; HRH = human resources for health.

Enhanced HRH Planning Functions

Table 7.2 shows 12 enhanced components that Eastern Caribbean countries should have in place to further support HRH strategic planning, but many are not yet in place.

Notes

1. Interview with Dominica's Chief Medical Officer, Dr. David Johnson, March 2014.
2. The literature review identified these as the four core components of HRH planning.

CHAPTER 8

Managing Human Resources for Health to Address Noncommunicable Diseases

Introduction

The proper implementation of human resources for health (HRH) management strategies can help overcome the health challenges that many countries face, and is critical for providing high-quality health care. Effective human resource management strategies are vital to achieve better outcomes from and greater access to health care. For noncommunicable diseases (NCDs), effective HRH management strategies are needed to ensure that stretched HRH resources are deployed where they can be most effective in delivering priority health care, and so begin to curb the impact of NCDs.

Core HRH Management Functions

The literature review identified six components of HRH management that need to be put in place to improve health service delivery: (1) a performance management system, (2) a standardized recruitment process, (3) opportunities for continuing professional development or in-service training, (4) a process for monitoring retention, (5) a process for succession planning, and (6) a process for evidence-based workforce planning. The combination of these six components can strengthen HRH management, which is needed to support HRH strategic planning efforts (table 8.1).

Performance Management System

While all four case study countries (Dominica, Grenada, St. Lucia, and St. Vincent and the Grenadines) conduct some form of review of employees in the public health sector, it is not clear whether this has an effect on performance. Three of the countries use a type of a public service appraisal tool that involves conducting annual reviews (Dominica) or semiannual

Table 8.1 Implementation of Core HRH Management Functions

Core HRH management functions	Dominica	Grenada	St. Lucia	St. Vincent and the Grenadines
Performance management system	Yes	In progress	Yes	In progress
Standardized process for recruitment	Yes	Yes	In progress	No
Opportunities for continuing professional development or in-service training	Yes	Yes	Yes	Yes
Process for monitoring retention	No	In progress	In progress	No
Process for succession planning	In progress	In progress	No	No
Process for evidence-based workforce planning	No	In progress	In progress	In progress

Source: Desk review and field interviews conducted in March 2014.
Note: HRH = human resources for health.

reviews (Grenada and St. Lucia). St. Vincent and the Grenadines does not have a formal performance evaluation system, although nurses are assessed by their supervisors at initially three-month, six-month, and one-year intervals, and subsequently on an annual basis. Although performance systems are in place and performance reviews are conducted, it is unclear how the results of these evaluations are being used to influence performance.

A report funded by the U.S. Agency for International Development (USAID) noted that feedback from managers on absenteeism and poor performance in Dominica, even if noted in performance reviews, had little impact on annual salary increases or job stability. In Grenada, the use of a generic public service tool for appraisals resulted in the omission of HRH-specific standards. St. Lucia is pilot testing a new performance appraisal system in four ministries, but not the Ministry of Health.

The four case study countries experience high rates of absenteeism in their health workforce. The combination of liberal leave policies and a complicated and lengthy disciplinary process, contributes to high rates of absenteeism among the health workforce. One manifestation of this is that health personnel take time off without securing replacements, leaving hospitals and clinics short-staffed. According to secondary data from field interviews, many nurses work far fewer than 40 hours a week, often leaving their clinics about midday. Community health aids are supposed to do home visits, but they seldom do because of a lack of oversight or penalties.

Recruitment

In all four case study countries, the recruitment and hiring process is lengthy, involving many steps and agencies. The ministry of health is involved in identifying needed posts and can be part of the initial vetting process, but each post must be approved by the public service commission. This is an intricate and protracted process that requires internal clearances within the ministry and the commission; in St. Lucia's case, it also requires cabinet approval. In Dominica, hiring candidates recommended by the Ministry of Health may take up to one week for approval by the Establishment, Personnel, and Training Department and four to six weeks for approval by the Public Service Commission, depending on meeting schedules and the extent of the candidate review. When an employee resigns in St. Vincent and the Grenadines, the Ministry of Finance requires that all vacation time accrued by the resigning employee be used before the Ministry of Health can hire a replacement. After this, the Ministry of Health requests approval from the Ministry of Finance for filling the position, and only then will the Public Service Commission advertise and search for someone to fill the slot. Stakeholders noted that requests for staff were typically made during the preparation of national budgets, resulting in the processing being hurried and lacking data support, thus hindering the ability of public service bodies to determine the validity of these requests.

Continuing Professional Development and Training
In-service training for technical and professional staff in the ministries of health in all four case study countries is available through the ministries and their collaborating agencies and organizations. In Dominica, the Establishment, Personnel, and Training Department is responsible for formal in-service training in the public sector. In Grenada, the hospital nursing service has a fully integrated in-service education program with nurses at St. George's Hospital having access to in-service training that covers, among other areas, clinical skills and management and staff appraisals. In Grenada and St. Lucia, ministries of health and the Pan American Health Organization offer in-service training on an array of topics, including disaster management, medical coding, maternal and child health, management of NCDs, water monitoring, and the management of dialysis patients. In-service training for nurses in St. Vincent and the Grenadines is organized by the medical director at Milton Cato Memorial Hospital; training covers, among other topics, clinical care and management skills. Lecturers from the Trinity School of Medicine often hold these seminars.

Several short-term training opportunities enhance the formal educational and in-service training offerings in the Eastern Caribbean. Medical and pharmacy councils offer continuing medical education training in partnership with provider associations. Grenada also benefits from short-term training opportunities regularly offered by St. George's University, and from an annual symposium that provides an opportunity to hear from overseas experts. For doctors, clinical teaching takes place every Friday at St. George's University Hospital in conjunction with St. George's University. In Dominica, Ross University School of Medicine is a key source of continuing education opportunities for HRH. The university offers monthly continuing medical education classes, weekly clinical practice presentations, and half-day research topics discussed two or three times a semester. The Ministry of Health can request specific continuing medical education topics, and it encourages public sector health workers to attend these classes. About 80–100 medical professionals attend the monthly continuing medical education sessions; Ross University provides certification of attendance.

Online courses are widening the scope for continuous professional education in Dominica and the other case study countries (before online courses, most medical professionals from the region would have had to attend courses abroad).

Despite the availability of in-service and continuing education opportunities for HRH in the Eastern Caribbean, there are challenges over inducting doctors and time constraints. Dominica has long had an induction program that integrates new hires into the system, provides close technical supportive supervision, and ensures that any gaps in training are addressed. Although the induction program is officially still in place, it is not functional and lacks leadership and guidance. In St. Lucia, several opportunities for in-service professional development exist, but staff shortages make it difficult to release staff from their duties to attend training. St. Lucia does not have an HRH training plan, but a hiring freeze, inadequate numbers of technical staff, and the growing burden of NCDs all call for development of a comprehensive HRH training plan. The Ministry of Health is also moving toward fully integrated primary health care, and this requires that staff receive training in knowledge and skills in this area.

Monitoring Retention

No formal mechanism is in place for monitoring retention across the four case study countries. Dominica, however, expects to have one once its HRH management databases are online. Grenada has minimal information on staff retention rates. Some data on an employee's reasons for leaving the Ministry of Health is captured in the human resource management module of SmartStream, an electronic human resources tracking system administered by the Public Service Commission. St. Lucia reports that its human resources retention rates are relatively stable, especially at the primary care level.

As well as tracking workforce flow, monitoring retention also captures how satisfied employees are in their work. Satisfaction surveys can also be used to identify challenges that affect HRH performance or workers leaving the health sector. Dominica does not use satisfaction surveys, but the government acknowledges they can be an important tool to get feedback on issues affecting employee performance and retention. Retention plans can enable a better staff response to the workplace experience, not only making it better and more fulfilling, but also helping retain essential personnel.

Since the 1980s, the migration of nurses from the Caribbean has at times been an issue, though it is not one currently because governments in the region brought in nurses from other countries to fill staffing gaps. Migration levels are affected by demand for nurses in other countries and the region's own economic situation (even major hurricanes can affect migration levels if they hit the economy). From 2003 to 2005, many nurses, especially those trained in specialized areas, and nursing trainers left their countries of origin for better opportunities. In response to the shortage, governments brought in nursing trainers from abroad, primarily from Cuba. In Dominica, this strategy led to more than 100 local nurses being trained from 2004 to 2007, which helped fill the staffing gap caused by migration.

Although data indicates the migration of nurses has declined over the past several years, the consensus among managers is that this is temporary. Currently, a large cohort of young nurses does not have the necessary experience to seek job opportunities in developed countries, but migration is expected to increase again once they gain that experience. To reduce attrition rates, Dominica raised the mandatory retirement age for nurses and nurse trainers from 55 to 60 years, which should ensure a more balanced nursing workforce of experienced and less-experienced nurses.

The attrition of health workers already practicing in the public sector puts pressure on retention strategies and monitoring efforts. In Dominica, the attrition of doctors practicing in the public sector is because of a preference for full-time private practice at home rather than a job abroad. Meanwhile, foreign doctors working in Dominica, especially specialists, tend to stay for a short time before moving on. Most migration of Dominican doctors happens after they have completed training (except for those trained in Cuba), and so they do not enter the public sector health workforce in the first place.

Succession Planning

Planning for the retirement of medical personnel is a must for maintaining programming continuity. Overall, all four case study countries lack succession planning, and none has a systematic method to forecast the demand for new and replacement HRH. Even so, Dominica is scaling up its SmartStream payroll software into a full-fledged human resources information system by including modules that can track training and conduct succession planning. The only reliable data in Grenada that can be used for succession planning are also in a SmartStream database, set up to support salary processing rather than human resources management. That said, the system now keeps track of pending retirements and why medical personnel left the public health sector. St. Lucia has no formal succession plan, but department heads informally let staff know of staffing needs and motivate them to pursue specialty training if there are shortages in certain areas. Such issues are discussed during biannual staff performance assessments.

Although succession planning needs to be strengthened, it is also critical for minister of health to be involved in the process to ensure that nurses are available to replace those nearing retirement, and that the same level of training and expertise is reflected in the next generation of nurses.

Workforce Planning

Workforce planning—which is not in place in any of the four case study countries—ties into both succession and retention planning. Staffing gaps are primarily found in nursing and medical specialist positions but, in the absence of an HRH strategic plan or a needs analysis, workforce planning is generally based on historical assumptions. Progress, however, is being made: a recent job audit and a planned workload analysis conducted in Dominica should help improve the HRH workforce planning process there. In 2010,

Table 8.2 Implementation Status of Enhanced HRH Management Functions

Enhanced HRH management functions	Dominica	Grenada	St. Lucia	St. Vincent and the Grenadines
Human resources manual/employee handbook	Yes	No	No	No
Review process to ensure policies and procedures are legally compliant	—	—	No	—
Process to ensure employee awareness of all policies and procedures	Yes	In progress	No	—
Annual review of legislative policies and procedures with employees	No	No	No	—
Employee acknowledgement form in employee handbook or human resource manual	—	—	—	—
Process in place to ensure adherence to all policies a practices	No	—	No	—
Policies and procedures written to ensure everyone has a clear understanding of the content	—	—	No	—
Employee satisfaction survey conducted	No	Yes	No	—

Source: Desk review and field interviews conducted in March 2014.
Note: — = not available; HRH = human resources for health.

St. Lucia completed a baseline assessment of national HRH and secured support from the Commonwealth Secretariat for workforce planning and policy development. The assessment concluded that the number of HRH staff was inadequate, and that redeployment and modification of job descriptions should be undertaken. In St. Vincent and the Grenadines, percentage increases in budgets guide the recruitment of new staff. Although the Ministry of Health has no HRH management and planning functions, these are split between the chief nursing officer, the chief medical officer, and the ministry's health planner.

Based on Grenada's recent human resource audit, the following actions were recommended for workforce planning: rationalizing HRH needs by realigning some services and promoting multitasking; and having all staff increases supported by empirical data and job analyses, and reviewed by the Department of Public Administration. For hospitals, the actual use of their services or the average occupancy rate should be a major factor for determining staffing levels and justifying any increases.

Enhanced HRH Management Functions

Once the core components for HRH management are implemented, the enhanced components become essential. As table 8.2 shows, countries should have in place eight enhanced components to further support HRH management, but, as of writing, many are not yet in place.

CHAPTER 9

Toolkit, Conclusions, and Recommendations

Toolkit

The toolkit was developed as a way to better address the increase in noncommunicable diseases (NCDs). The toolkit is based on the findings of this study and aims to provide Eastern Caribbean countries with resources to strengthen the planning and management of human resources for health (HRH). It comprises the following:

- A core dataset for developing an HRH information system (appendix C)
- A terms of reference template and discussion outline for an HRH multisector taskforce (appendix D)
- A toolkit to support evidence-based medicine (appendix E)
- A toolkit to support interprofessional team working (appendix F)
- A toolkit to support patient-centered care (appendix G)
- A toolkit for using informatics (appendix H)
- A toolkit for supporting quality improvement (appendix I)

Conclusions and Recommendations

Eastern Caribbean countries must adopt a strategic approach if they are to cope with the rise in NCDs and effectively manage the region's changing epidemiological profile. Drawing on research conducted by the Pan American Health Organization and the U.S. Agency for International Development (USAID), as well as the World Bank's gap analysis, it can be said that the quantity of medical personnel, particularly of primary care nurses, in the Eastern Caribbean is generally adequate. The gap is in the availability of nurses with specialization training.

Closing the gap will entail managing the workforce better and improving access to education and training opportunities in needed specializations. It will also entail improving HRH governance at country and regional levels. This, in turn, requires that countries have an HRH strategy that aligns with their national

The Nurse Workforce in the Eastern Caribbean • http://dx.doi.org/10.1596/978-1-4648-0830-2   43

health plans, so that adequate quantities and skill sets of human resources are in place to address national health priorities. Systems must also be established to effectively manage the performance of existing personnel.

The following are recommendations for nursing education, and management and planning, based on the findings from the regional analysis and the four country case studies:

Nursing Education

- *Better access to specialization training.* This is needed to manage and combat NCDs. Dominica's bachelor of science in nursing program received 60 applications for 20–40 available positions, which highlights the challenge that Eastern Caribbean countries face in being able to enroll all interested students into specialized nursing training. Strategies to increase access can include working with existing nursing programs to offer specialization training at the country level, bringing in professionals from other countries to teach specialized areas to compensate for faculty shortages, and working with the University of the West Indies and other regional universities to make specialization training more affordable and accessible. East Caribbean countries are already offering incentives to encourage nurses to specialize. St. Lucia offers study leave to nurses pursuing a bachelor's or master's degree by providing 100 percent of their salary during the first year and 75 percent during the second year; the government also pays for a portion of the tuition costs for students who pass the courses and agree to return and work in the public sector. St. Vincent and the Grenadines follows a similar approach, providing study leave for nurses pursuing specialization training equivalent to full salary for the first year and 50 percent for the second year; graduates are also hired at a higher pay grade if they do specialization training.

- *Increase educational offerings, scholarships, and incentives.* To counter the high cost of pursuing additional education, more educational offerings should be available in country, scholarships should be available to make training more affordable, and incentives should be in place to reward nurses who invest the time and expense to acquire additional training. Many Eastern Caribbean countries already have a tuition reimbursement program for nurses seeking higher education (bachelor's or master's degrees). While this is helpful, these programs usually require nurses to work for five years before being eligible for this assistance. Many nurses have started a family by then, and the reimbursement does not cover the expense of relocating their families.

- *Include customer service skills and patient-centered care in the nursing curriculum to ensure that nurses are treating patients with respect.* Combating NCDs requires that patients comply in the treatment of their disease. If they feel disrespected by nurses, they will be less likely to seek medical treatment, which can reduce country health outcomes. The University of the West Indies is the main source of postgraduate training for NCDs. At the university's four campuses, 63 courses were offered in 23 subjects in the 2013/14 academic year that were relevant to primary and tertiary care, and NCDs.

- *Offer management and human resources training specific to health at universities or community colleges.* The Eastern Caribbean suffers from a deficit of HRH management skills. Without educational offerings it will be difficult for ministries of health to find staff with the needed skills.

- *Ministries of health should track health workers attending short-term training to make the best use of trained personnel.* In 2014, Dominica determined that 80–100 health workers attended continuing training, which highlights the high demand for further training. Oversight on nurses attending training is needed to ensure that younger nurses, who need it most, are attending courses and workshops.

Management and Planning
- *Increase control of health personnel.* Ministries of health need to have greater control over their personnel, particularly in hiring and firing, to prevent hiring delays and ensure that those being hired are the best qualified candidates. The region's centralized government structure, which has a separate entity (usually a public service commission) to manage hiring and firing, does create a system of checks and balances. But this also results in hiring delays and is inefficient, to the extent that those conducting interviews often lack the technical expertise to evaluate candidates effectively.
- *Tackle absenteeism.* Absenteeism results in shortages at clinics and hospitals, even though the levels of HRH on the payroll may appear to be sufficient. This is particularly the case in Grenada. Better management of nursing staff is needed to ensure that absenteeism has repercussions, and that time off is handled in a way that does not jeopardize coverage at hospitals and clinics.
- *Put in place a mobility plan to encourage specialized training.* A clear plan is needed for mobility within the clinical setting to incentivize nurses to get specialist training. Incentives for nurses with specialized training are needed to encourage more nurses to incur the cost and time of further education. At present, nurses are not automatically given a pay increase or promotion if they do specialized training.
- *Put in place the core and essential components for strategic HRH management and planning.* This includes a health information management system and a definite HRH plan.

Country Case Studies

Introduction

Dominica, Grenada, St. Lucia, and St. Vincent and the Grenadines were the four Eastern Caribbean countries selected for this report's case studies. This section provides a demographic overview of each country, a human resources for health (HRH) profile for combatting noncommunicable diseases (NCD), and a gap analysis for the key components for HRH management and planning. The main HRH components of each national HRH response are stratified into HRH planning (core and enhanced) and HRH management (core and enhanced). Core components should be fully implemented before enhanced components are initiated.

Country Benchmarks

Understanding the performance of key health indicators in the four case study countries compared to other Caribbean countries makes it possible to see where the four have achieved success in health and where they are lagging. Tables A.1 and A.2 list 15 Caribbean countries, ranking them in relation to five metrics of interest in which 1 is the highest rank and 15 the lowest. Age-standardized rates are used to make meaningful comparisons across time by adjusting for changes in population size and age structure. Life expectancy incorporates mortality; health-adjusted life expectancy incorporates years lived in less-than-ideal health. The four case study countries are highlighted in gray.

Table A.1 Age-Standardized Death Rate, YLL, and YLD Indicators, Selected Caribbean Countries, 1990 and 2010

Country	Age-standardized death rate (per 100,000 population) 1990 Rate	1990 Rank	2010 Rate	2010 Rank	Age-standardized YLL rate (per 100,000 population) 1990 Rate	1990 Rank	2010 Rate	2010 Rank	Age-standardized YLD rate (per 100,000 population) 1990 Rate	1990 Rank	2010 Rate	2010 Rank
Antigua and Barbuda	728	3	593	3	19,168	3	13,919	2	12,425	4	13,535	12
Bahamas, The	949	13	541	1	29,297	13	18,258	6	13,220	11	12,791	4
Barbados	744	4	593	4	21,168	5	15,643	3	12,700	7	12,588	2
Belize	765	5	805	11	20,556	4	21,887	13	12,951	9	13,377	11
Cuba	635	1	543	2	15,919	1	11,088	1	11,765	1	12,791	3
Dominica	831	7	669	6	24,475	7	19,240	8	12,486	6	13,022	8
Dominican Republic	765	6	683	7	23,701	6	18,385	7	12,154	3	12,232	1
Grenada	904	10	850	12	25,983	10	21,313	11	13,149	10	13,076	10
Guyana	1,199	14	1,124	14	35,469	14	31,305	14	13,663	14	14,024	13
Haiti	1,717	15	3,321	15	61,823	15	137,295	15	15,059	15	16,428	15
Jamaica	676	2	610	5	18,618	2	16,417	4	12,075	2	12,909	6
St. Lucia	891	9	722	9	25,875	9	17,785	5	13,328	13	14,233	14
St. Vincent and the Grenadines	890	8	753	10	26,567	11	20,602	9	13,233	12	13,056	9
Suriname	922	11	693	8	27,022	12	20,892	10	12,827	8	12,945	7
Trinidad and Tobago	934	12	883	13	24,788	8	21,845	12	12,458	5	12,885	5

Source: World Bank, World DataBank.
Note: YLDs = years lived with disability; YLLs = years of life lost.

Table A.2 Life Expectancy at Birth Indicators, Selected Caribbean Countries, 1990 and 2010

Country	Life expectancy at birth (years)				Health-adjusted life expectancy at birth (years)			
	1990		2010		1990		2010	
	Rate	Rank	Rate	Rank	Rate	Rank	Rate	Rank
Antigua and Barbuda	73.1	3	76.5	2	62.7	3	63.3	2
Bahamas, The	67.4	13	76	3	57.4	13	63.2	4
Barbados	71.9	5	75.6	4	61.4	4	63.3	3
Belize	72	4	71.2	11	61.2	5	59.4	12
Cuba	74.8	1	77.9	1	64.6	1	65.2	1
Dominica	70.3	7	73.8	6	60.2	7	61.5	8
Dominican Republic	70.8	6	73.7	7	60.9	6	62.2	6
Grenada	68.9	9	71	12	58.7	9	59.6	11
Guyana	64.1	14	66	14	54.6	14	55	14
Haiti	54.1	15	37.2	15	45.7	15	31.8	15
Jamaica	73.6	2	75.3	5	63.2	2	62.8	5
St. Lucia	68.9	10	73.7	8	58.6	10	61.6	7
St. Vincent and the Grenadines	68.7	11	72	10	58.5	12	60.2	10
Suriname	68.5	12	72.6	9	58.6	11	60.7	9
Trinidad and Tobago	69.1	8	70.6	13	59.5	8	59.4	13

Source: World Bank, World DataBank.

Dominica

Demographic Overview

Dominica, an island in the Eastern Caribbean, has a total land area of 751 square kilometers and comprises 10 administrative parishes (map A.1). The United Nations Human Development Index, a standard measure of human development, focusing on education, health care, income, and employment, ranks Dominica 72 out of 178 countries for human development (UNDP 2013).

Dominica's population is just over 71,000, according to the most recent census in 2011. The population has been fairly static, rising from 70,928 in 1990 to 71,167 in 2010 for an absolute population increase of 248 and a percentage increase of 0.3 percent. The population density (population per square kilometer) was 94.4 in 1990 and 94.8 in 2010; the Caribbean's average population density was 146.2 in 1990 and 177.6 in 2010 (UNDP 2013).

Health Care System

Dominica's health care delivery system is based on a primary health care model that includes both primary and secondary health care. Tertiary care is not offered in country, and patients are referred to facilities in neighboring countries. The country is divided into two administrative regions and seven health districts. Primary health care is decentralized to the district level, and provided for free through a network of 52 primary care clinics. Secondary health care is provided at two district hospitals, but it is not free. In addition to free primary care, the government covers health care costs for all Dominican residents ages 18 and younger and 65 and older.[1]

Health Profile and NCD Burden

Life expectancy in Dominica rose from 70.3 years in 1990 to 73.8 years in 2010; health-adjusted life expectancy rose from 60.2 years to 61.5 years in the same period. The age-standardized mortality rate for all causes in 1990 was 831 per 100,000 population, and it had fallen to 669 by 2010, a decrease of 19.5 percent.

Map A.1 Dominica's 10 Parishes

The largest reductions in mortality for all causes over this period was in older age groups, with smaller reductions (and sometimes increases) among young adults. The largest reduction in mortality rates for all causes was for women ages 50–54 (49 percent). The largest increase in mortality rates (20 percent) was for males ages 30–34 (UNDESA 2013).

For years of life lost (YLLs), a measure quantifying premature mortality by weighting younger deaths more than older deaths, the top five causes of premature death in Dominica in 2010 were ischemic heart disease (800 YLLs, 6 percent of total YLLs); stroke (700 YLLs, 5.6 percent of total YLLs); diabetes (700 YLLs, 5.4 percent of total YLLs); preterm birth complications (600 YLLs, 4.5 percent of total YLLs); and lower respiratory infections (500 YLLs, 4.3 percent of total YLLs). Changes in the 20 years since 1990 in the leading five causes were ischemic heart disease (10 percent reduction), stroke (10 percent reduction), diabetes (30 percent increase), preterm birth complications (62 percent reduction), and lower respiratory infections (45 percent reduction) (IHME 2013).

Of the top 25 causes of premature mortality, 15 have shown reductions, and eight have shown increases of 25 percent or greater between 1990 and 2010. On the rise were diabetes (5.4 percent of total YLLs, 30 percent increase); prostate cancer (3 percent of total YLLs, 79 percent increase); interpersonal violence (1.8 percent of total YLLs, 108 percent increase); chronic kidney disease (1.7 percent of total YLLs, 46 percent increase); cardiomyopathy (1.4 percent of total YLLs, 112 percent increase); pancreatic cancer (1.4 percent of total YLLs, 25 percent increase); colorectal cancer (1.1 percent of total YLLs, 161 percent increase); and self-harm (1.1 percent of total YLLs, 88 percent increase) (IHME 2013).

The five leading causes of years lived with disability (YLDs), estimated by weighting the prevalence of different conditions based on severity, in Dominica are major depressive disorder, lower back pain, iron-deficiency anemia, diabetes mellitus, and the adverse effects of medical treatment (IHME 2013).

Disability-adjusted life years (DALYs) quantify both YLLs and YLDs within a population. In Dominica, the top three causes of DALYs in 2010 were diabetes mellitus, ischemic heart disease, and major depressive disorder. Two causes that appeared in the 10 leading causes of DALYs in 2010 but not in 1990 were lower back pain and prostate cancer (IHME 2013). Of the 25 most important causes of disease burden measured by DALYs, preterm birth complications showed the largest decrease, falling 61 percent from 1990 to 2010. The leading risk factor was high blood pressure (IHME 2013).

Overall, the three risk factors that account for the greatest disease burden in Dominica are high blood pressure, dietary risks, and high body mass index. The leading risk factors in 2010 for children ages under five and adults ages 15–49 were suboptimal breastfeeding and alcohol use, respectively.

Dominica faces a rise in NCDs with the leading causes of death attributed to diabetes, stroke, hypertension, prostate cancer, and acute respiratory infection.[2] Diabetes directly affects 17.7 percent of the population (12.3 percent female, 21.8 percent male).[3] Hypertension is a concern, with 32.1 percent of the population experiencing raised blood pressure.[4]

Of the four major NCD groups (cancer, cerebrovascular disease, cardiac disease, diabetes), three are the leading causes of morbidity and mortality in Dominica. An analysis of visits to district medical officers and family nurse practitioners between 1999 and 2005 found 22 percent of visits were due to hypertension, and 13 percent were due to diabetes (Abt Associates 2012a). The increasing NCD burden poses additional challenges in Dominica by raising the prevalence of serious complications, such as amputations, cardiovascular events, and diabetic retinopathy and blindness.

Cancer
Compared to other malignant neoplasms, YLLs due to prostate, pancreatic, and colorectal cancer rose significantly in Dominica in the last 20 years (increases of 79 percent, 25 percent, and 161 percent, respectively). It is interesting to note that prostate cancer only appeared as a significant cause of DALYs in 2010. When undertaking workforce planning it is worth considering the importance of bringing on board medical specialists such as oncologists (and possibly urologists), along with the relevant allied professionals that will provide palliative and rehabilitative care for these conditions (UNDESA 2013).

Cerebrovascular Disease
Between 1990 and 2010, YLLs due to stroke declined 10 percent, though stroke remain the second highest cause of premature mortality. This suggests the need for strengthening capacity for diagnosing and managing stroke in an emergency setting, as well as for raising awareness of the symptoms of stroke onset, so that medical assistance can be sought as soon as possible. For stroke survivors, intensive rehabilitation needs to be provided, but Dominica has only four rehabilitation specialists (UNDESA 2013).

Cardiac Disease
Between 1990 and 2010, YLLs due to ischemic heart disease dropped 10 percent, although ischemic heart disease remained the second leading cause of DALYs in 2010. In the same period, cardiomyopathy increased 112 percent.

Diabetes
YLLs due to diabetes increased 30 percent between 1990 and 2010, and this was one the leading five causes of YLDs and the leading cause of DALYs in 2010. Despite this, Dominica's public health sector has no medical specialists to manage this disease. Diabetes and two of its three leading risk factors (dietary risks and high body mass index) require changes in patterns of nutrition for its management and prevention to be successful. Dominica, however, has only one registered nutritionist (UNDESA 2013).

Gap Analysis for HRH Planning and Management to Combat NCDs
According to Pan American Health Organization (PAHO) data, Dominica's overall health worker density is adequate compared to the regional average.

More specifically, the density of doctors and nurses is adequate compared to the Caribbean baseline. However, Dominica's density of primary care physicians and specialists is not optimal. Although most of its primary health care workforce has some public health skills, the country needs to increase the number of physicians in its primary health care system. Careful consideration should also be given to the skill sets and competencies that any additional physicians should have. Prince Margaret Hospital employs some 58 percent of the country's public health sector workers, making it the largest employer of health workers.

Concern over access to primary health care services in Dominica is growing amid demographic shifts. Large new communities are developing, creating an imbalance in the demand and use of primary health care services. Consequently, Dominica's health districts and shift resources may need to be redefined to meet these changing demands.

According to PAHO guidelines, Dominica has enough primary care nurses, although the country wants to hire more. As of latest data for 2014,[5] Dominica had 419 nursing positions, 358 of which were filled (including nurses working in temporary positions); 293 of these nurses are working in primary care, and less than 1 percent are foreign.

According to interviews with government officials, the country's main HRH challenge is a shortage of nurses with specific skills and specialty training. Dominica, for example, has only one neonatal nurse. The shortage is particularly noticeably for nurses and medical officers specializing in gynecology, general surgery, pathology, anesthesiology, cardiology, intensive care nursing, operating and surgery, ophthalmology, and pediatric nursing. The country also has a shortage of midwives, partly because before being trained as a midwife, a nurse must be a registered nurse. Because the region as a whole is experiencing a scarcity of specialists, Dominica is looking to recruit more specialists from abroad, including from the Philippines. Dominica already brings in specialists from other countries, including doctors from China and doctors, specialist nurses, and intensive care nurses from Cuba.

The private sector also recruits nurses, with a small number (exact figures are not available) working in doctors' offices and homes for the elderly. Benefits and pay are slightly better in the private sector. Most health personnel who work in the private sector also work for the public sector.

Dominica's staffing profile (table A.3) does not match the requirements indicated by its current or predicted NCD profile.

Legislation Affecting HRH Planning

Table A.4 lists Dominica's legislative statutes that affect HRH planning. The main legislative gap is health and safety.

Other legislation relevant to HRH planning includes the Labour Standards Act, Mental Health Act, Public Service Act, Environmental Health Services Act, General Orders and Public Service Commission Regulations, Hospitals and Health Care Facilities Act, Roseau Hospital Ordinance Act, Roseau Hospital Rules, and the Accreditation Act.

Table A.3 HRH Staffing Profile for Treating NCDs, Dominica

Number of HRH by key NCD professional category (2008)		
Professional category	Total (no.)	Density (per 10,000 population)
Doctors	124	17.1
Nurses and midwives	370	50.9
Nurses, midwives, nursing assistants	562	77.3
Rehabilitation specialists	4	0.6
Nutritionists	1	0.1
Doctors, nurses, midwives	494	68.0
All health care providers	739	101.7
All health workers	824	113.4
Staff in community health	198	
Medical specialists[a]	21	
Specialist type		
Cardiologists	0	
Rehabilitation specialists	0	
Neurologists	0	
Oncologists	0	
Pathologists	1	
Radiologists	1	

HRH targets related to chronic NCD management (2011)		
Description	Target	Level of progress
HRH density per 10,000 population	25	100 percent of target achieved
Primary health care teams with broad range of skills	—	100 percent of target achieved
Proportion of doctors in primary health care	40 percent	35 percent of target achieved (27 primary health care physicians)
Proportion of workers with public health skills	70 percent	70 percent of target achieved
Proportion of managers with public health skills	60 percent	78 percent of target achieved

Source: Information collected by the Pan American Health Organization from 2008 to 2012 as part of the Regional Goals for Human Resources for Health 2007–15 initiative.
Note: — = not available; HRH = human resources for health; NCD = noncommunicable disease.
a. Senior medical doctors at Princess Margaret Hospital by specialty: anesthesia (2); consultant physician (1); internal medicine (1); gynecology (3); ophthalmology (1); pediatrics (2); pathology (1); radiology (2); general surgery (2); orthopedic surgery (1); ear, nose, throat (1); intensive care (3); gastroenterology (1).

Core Components for Strategic HRH Planning and Management

The four core components for strategic HRH planning and management are a national health plan, an HRH management unit or function within the ministry of health, an HRH information system, and a multisector HRH taskforce. Dominica has a national health plan in place and is working on establishing an HRH information system.

The country has no formal HRH policy, although developing one has been under discussion for many years. The Ministry of Health's leadership wants to develop an HRH policy that aligns with its strategic plan,[7] but progress has stalled because of the lack of a champion to make this a priority and budgetary constraints, as well as personnel, expertise, and government structure issues.

Table A.4 Legislation Related to HRH Planning, Dominica

Legislation area	Exists	Legislation and statutes	
Legislation covering essential services	Yes	Essential Services Act	
Legislation covering trade union formation and industrial relations	Yes	Labour Code Trade Union Act Industrial Relations Act	
Legislation covering health and safety	No	In the absence of legislation regarding the health and safety of workers, Dominica relies on the Employment Safety Act and Factory and Machinery Rules	
Legislation covering registration of health professionals	Yes		
Nurses and midwives			Midwifery Rules (1936) Midwifery Ordinance (1931) Nurses Registration Act (2005)
Doctors, pharmacists, dentists, and opticians			Medical Act (1990)

Source: National legislation and statutes.
Note: HRH = human resources for health.

National Health Plan—In Place

The public health sector is guided by the National Strategic Plan for Health 2010–19. This encompasses a health situation analysis, a population's health and disease profile, and an action plan identifying needs and priorities in health interventions.

HRH Management Unit—Not in Place

In Dominica's highly centralized governmental structure, HRH are managed by the Establishment, Personnel, and Training Department within the Ministry of National Security. Hiring is officially done through the Public Service Commission, although the Ministry of Health participates in interviewing applicants and submitting hiring requests to the department, which then issues a recommendation to the commission. This process was set up to create a system of checks and balances, but the planning and management of health care personnel has been undermined by keeping the human resource function outside the Ministry of Health. Administrative officers within the Ministry of Health handle general human resource matters such as managing vacation time and keeping track of pending retirements. But the ministry has no resources to undertake more strategic human resource issues, such as recruitment, retention, and training, that can help meet the country's health needs.

HRH Information System—In Progress

The Establishment, Personnel, and Training Department's database collects only limited HRH data, such as employee biographic information including skills and competencies. The department is in the process of scaling up its SmartStream payroll software into a full-fledged human-resource information system by adding modules that can track training and be used for succession planning. The Ministry of Health is given access to the department's data if it requests it, but, at this juncture, access is not shared. The ministry will eventually have direct access (read only) to the SmartStream software for internal human resource planning and management. In the meantime, a Microsoft-based database into which the ministry can record personnel information of its employees is being used. This database, developed by the government's information and communication technology unit, is being populated with data from personnel records. It is unclear, however, how this standalone desktop database relates to SmartStream, or whether there will be any interaction between the two systems.

HRH Multisector Taskforce—Not in Place
Dominica does not have a multisector taskforce to address HRH issues.

Enhanced Components for HRH Planning
Table A.5 outlines the enhanced components for HRH planning and their implementation status in Dominica. The enhanced components are essential for HRH planning once the core components are in place.

Core HRH Management Functions
Table A.6 shows the status of the components and practices for HRH management in Dominica.

Performance Management—In Place
A report by the U.S. Agency for International Development (USAID) (Abt Associates 2012b) found that public sector employment policies did not maximize performance, despite an annual review process. Liberal leave policies coupled with

Table A.5 Status of Enhanced Components for Strategic HRH Planning, Dominica

Enhanced components	Exist
HRH plan	No
HRH leadership	Yes
HRH champion within the Ministry of Health	No
Process for aligning HRH planning to Ministry of Health needs	No
Process for aligning training needs to Ministry of Health requirements	No
Mechanism for coordinating activities between the private and public health sectors	No
Mechanism for coordinating activities between community organizations and the public health sector	No
HRH development and training plan	No
Financial and service delivery plan that balances reasonably expected health care resources and commitments	No
Human resources policies and procedures	In progress
Estimates of national health accounts	No

Note: HRH = human resources for health.

Table A.6 Status of Core Components and Practices for HRH Management, Dominica

Core components and practices	Exist
Performance management system	Yes
Standardized and transparent recruitment process	Yes
Opportunities for continuing professional development or in-service training	Yes
Process for monitoring retention	No
Process for succession planning	In progress
Process for evidence-based workforce planning	No

Note: HRH = human resources for health.

a complicated and lengthy disciplinary process contribute to high rates of absenteeism in the health workforce. The annual review process—the Employee Assessment and Development Review—is based on key result areas and performance objectives, and is also used to determine salary increases. Although use of the review process has increased, and has proved worthwhile for developing training plans, the extent of its use as a performance management tool is unclear. The USAID report suggests that feedback from some managers about problems related to absenteeism and poor performance indicates that actual employee performance, even if noted in the review, has little impact on annual salary increases or job stability.

Interviews with officials confirmed that the management and absenteeism of nurses is a concern in Dominica. Health personnel take time off without securing replacements, leaving hospital and clinics short-staffed. Many nurses work far fewer than 40 hours a week, often leaving work around midday. Moreover, community health aids do not do their required home visits, a situation created by lack of oversight and repercussions.

Recruitment—In Place

The Public Service Act and General Orders and Public Service Commission Regulations provide a framework for the recruitment process, which involves multiple agencies. Candidates are initially vetted by the Ministry of Health, which reviews applicants and conducts interviews. The permanent secretary then submits a recommendation to the Establishment, Personnel, and Training Department, which forwards it to the Public Service Commission. It can take up to one week for a candidacy recommended by the ministry to be approved by the department, and four to six weeks to get approved by the commission, depending on its meeting schedules and its review of the candidate.

Continuing Professional Development and Training—In Place

The Establishment, Personnel, and Training Department is responsible for in-service training in the public sector. Training opportunities for Ministry of Health technical or professional staff are offered by collaborating agencies and other entities.

Physicians historically have benefitted from an induction program that integrated new hires into the system, provided close technical support supervision, and ensured that any gaps in training were addressed. This program is officially still in place, but it is no longer functional and lacks leadership and guidance. Instead, medical staff at the Princess Margaret Hospital have a weekly forum at which presentations are made and cases discussed. The hospital nursing service has a fully integrated in-service education program. The General Nursing Council requires proof of continuing medical education as for license renewal.

Ross University School of Medicine offers continuing education opportunities for HRH. The university holds continuing medical education classes every third Friday of the month, weekly clinical practice presentations, and half-day research topics discussions held two or three times a semester. The Ministry of Health can request that specific topics for continuing medical education are covered, and it encourages public sector health workers to attend. About 80–100 people typically attend these sessions, and Ross University provides certification of attendance. Online courses further increased the scope for continuous medical education. Before online courses, most medical professionals had to go abroad to attend courses.

Monitoring Retention—Not in Place or in Progress

Dominica has no formal process for monitoring retention, although this will change when HRH management databases come online. As well as tracking the workforce flow, retention monitoring tracks employee satisfaction, whether challenges affect performance, and whether employees want to move outside of the sector. Dominica does not use an employee satisfaction survey, but this can be useful to understand the issues that affect employee performance and retention. Once a retention plan is in place, staff experiences can be better responded to, thus improving work experience and retaining essential personnel.

Monitoring retention is particularly important in a context in which migration is high and a country faces a loss of essential health personnel. By monitoring workforce flow, a country can proactively develop strategies to retain key personnel. Although migration has been a matter of concern for Dominica, this is not currently the case. Since the mid-1980s, the migration of Dominica's health personnel has ebbed and flowed, depending on the demand for nurses in other countries and Dominica's economic circumstances at any given time (even major hurricanes that have hit the economy have been a cause of migration).

Although the migration of nurses has declined in the past several years, managers believe this may be temporary. A large cohort of young nurses currently does not have the necessary experience to get jobs in developed countries, but this will change once they have the necessary experience, and migration is likely to increase again.

The attrition of doctors from the public sector is because of their preference for full-time employment in private practice, rather than migration. Foreign doctors, especially specialists, tend to stay in the public sector for a just a short time before moving on. Much of the migration of doctors occurs soon after they have completed training. Those trained in Cuba are the exception; in return for training, they agree to work back home for a number of years.

To reduce attrition rates in the nurse workforce, Dominica recently raised the mandatory retirement age for nurses and nursing trainers from 55 to 60; this should ensure a more balanced nursing workforce of experienced and less-experienced nurses.

Succession Planning—In Progress

Succession planning for HRH is not practiced in Dominica. The Establishment, Personnel, and Training Department, however, is working to add a module to its human resources information system for a succession plan. This will be an important advance once completed, but it is essential that the Ministry of Health is directly involved in the succession planning process to ensure enough nurses are in place to replace those nearing retirement, and that the same level of training and expertise is evident in the next generation of nurses.

Workforce Planning—Not in Place or in Progress

Workforce planning ties into both succession and retention planning, and is not in place for HRH in Dominica. Workforce planning is based on historical assumptions, although a recent job audit and a planned workload analysis should help improve the workforce planning process. Staffing gaps are primarily in nursing and medical specialist positions.

Enhanced Components and Practices for HRH Management

Table A.7 shows the enhanced components and practices for HRH management that have been put in place, and those that still need to be implemented.

On being hired, nurses go through an orientation process and receive a clinical procedures training manual. During orientation, the Establishment, Personnel, and Training Department is invited to speak on human resource rules, policies, and procedures. Instruction on the training manual is conducted at Princess Margaret Hospital, but nurses do not receive an individual copy of the manual. While supervisors are in place, no structured process exists to ensure adherence to policies and practices. And as previously noted, employee satisfaction surveys are not conducted.

Table A.7 Status of Enhanced Components and Practices for HRH Management, Dominica

Enhanced components and practices	Exists
Human resources manual or employee handbook with employee acknowledgement form	Yes
Process to ensure employee awareness of all policies and procedures	Yes
Review process to ensure policies and procedures are legally compliant	Unknown
Annual review of legislative policies and procedures with employees	No
Process in place to ensure adherence to all policies and practices	No
Policies and procedures written to ensure employees have a clear understanding of the content	Unknown
Employee satisfaction survey conducted	No

Note: HRH = human resources for health.

Grenada

Demographic Overview

Grenada is an upper middle-income country in the southeastern Caribbean (map A.2). The land area of its three main islands—Grenada, Carriacou, and Petite Martinique—and six smaller islands covers 344 square kilometers, and is divided into seven administrative parishes (six in Grenada and one in Carriacou). The United Nations Human Development Index ranks Grenada 63 out of 178 countries (UNDP 2013).

Grenada's population was 105,500 as of the 2012 census. The population has increased gradually, rising from 96,286 in 1990 to 104,677 in 2010 for an absolute population increase of 8,391 and a percentage increase of 8.7 percent. The population density (population per square meter) was 279.9 in 1990 and 304.3 in 2010; the Caribbean's average population density was 146.2 in 1990 and 177.6 in 2010 (UNDESA 2013).

Health Care System

Grenada is divided into seven health districts,[8] which have 36 health facilities, comprising 30 medical stations and six health centers. Grenada also has four public and two private hospitals. Medical stations are located every six miles (9.7 kilometers) to ensure widespread access to care, and are staffed by a district nurse, community health nurses, nurse aids, and a caretaker. A doctor provides care at these stations once a week. Health centers include specialty clinics, and each one has a public health nurse in charge of the district.[9]

Grenada offers primary, secondary, and tertiary care, although some people still seek treatment abroad, especially for cancer. Primary care is free and there are no user fees to see a doctor or nurse, but laboratory work, X-rays, pharmaceuticals, and beds are charged for. Because of rising health care costs, however, Grenada is exploring the introduction of fees. The government recently enacted

Map A.2 The Six Parishes of the Main Island of Grenada

reforms to revitalize primary care by extending opening hours at medical stations. The health system is primarily funded by government revenue, and
8.6 percent of the overall budget is allocated to health care.[10]

Health Profile and NCD Burden

Life expectancy in Grenada rose from 68.9 years in 1990 to 71.0 years in 2010,
and health-adjusted life expectancy rose from 58.7 years to 59.6 in the same
period. The age-standardized mortality rate for all causes in 1990 was 904 per
100,000 population, falling to 850 per 100,000 in 2010. The largest reductions
in mortality for all causes in that period were among the youngest age groups;
the smaller reductions (and sometimes increases) were among young adults.
The largest reductions in mortality rates for all causes were among females ages
1–4 (67 percent). Males ages 35–39 years experienced the largest increases
(19 percent) (UNDESA 2013).

For YLLs due to premature death, ischemic heart disease, cerebrovascular
disease, and diabetes mellitus were the leading causes in Grenada in 2010. Of the
25 most important causes of disease burden, as measured by DALYs, preterm
birth complications showed the largest decrease, falling by 70 percent from 1990
to 2010. The leading risk factor is dietary risks (IHME 2013).

In 2010, the top five causes of premature death in Grenada were ischemic
heart disease (1,800 YLLs, 9 percent of total YLLs); stroke (1,500 YLLs,
7.5 percent of total YLLs); diabetes (1300 YLLs, 6.2 percent of total YLLs);
lower respiratory infections (900 YLLs, 4.7 percent of total YLLs); and other
cardio and circulatory diseases (700 YLLs, 3.4 percent of total YLLs). Changes in
the 20 years since 1990 for the top five causes were ischemic heart disease
(17 percent reduction), stroke (37 percent reduction), diabetes (122 percent
increase), lower respiratory infections (64 percent reduction), other cardio and
circulatory diseases (12 percent reduction) (IHME 2013).

Of the top 25 causes of premature mortality, nine have shown reductions and
12 have shown increases of 25 percent or greater between 1990 and 2010.
Among those on the rise were diabetes (6.2 percent of total YLLs, 122 percent
increase); hypertensive heart disease (1.8 percent of total YLLs, 60 percent
increase); and drug use disorders (1.2 percent of total YLLs, 54 percent increase)
(IHME 2013).

The five leading causes of YLDs in Grenada are major depressive disorder,
lower back pain, iron-deficiency anemia, diabetes mellitus, and neck pain (IHME
2013).

The top three causes of DALYs in Grenada in 2010 were ischemic heart disease, diabetes mellitus, and cerebrovascular disease. Causes that were among the
top 10 in 2010 but not in 1990 were road injury, lower back pain, and other
musculoskeletal disorders (IHME 2013).

Overall, the three risk factors that account for most of the disease burden in
Grenada are dietary risks, high blood pressure, and high body mass index. The
leading risk factors in 2010 for children ages under five and adults ages 15–49
were suboptimal breastfeeding and alcohol use, respectively (IHME 2013).

Of the four NCDs (cancer, cerebrovascular disease, cardiac disease, diabetes), three are the leading causes of premature mortality in Grenada. The Ministry of Health's approach in addressing NCDs focuses on clinical care and treatment. Monthly chronic disease clinics emphasizing the management of diabetes and hypertension are conducted by staff at community health facilities. Some facilities report that interest in these clinics is low (Abt Associates 2012b).

Cancer

Cancer is the country's leading cause of death, followed by metabolic conditions such as diabetes, cardiovascular disease, hypertension, and stroke.[11] Of the various malignant neoplasms, YLLs due to prostate, liver, breast, and colorectal cancer have increased significantly in the last 20 years (73 percent, 97 percent, 155 percent, and 60 percent, respectively). Premature deaths due to non-Hodgkin's lymphoma increased by 68 percent in the same period.

When conducting workforce planning, it is worth considering the integration of medical specialists such as radiation oncologists, pathologists, and possibly urologists, along with the standard allied professionals for the provision of palliative and rehabilitation care (PAHO 2013).

Cerebrovascular Disease

Between 1990 and 2010, YLLs due to stroke decreased 37 percent, although stroke remained the third highest cause of DALYs in 2010. This suggests an improvement in diagnosing and managing stroke in an emergency setting. Even so, HRH awareness of the symptoms of stroke onset need to be raised so that medical assistance can be sought as soon as possible. Because stroke remains a leading cause of death, an increase in the capacity of HRH to manage this condition should be considered (PAHO 2013).

Cardiac Disease

In the two decades before 2010, YLLs due to ischemic heart disease decreased 17 percent, although this condition remained the highest cause of premature death and DALYs in 2010. Hypertensive heart disease increased by 60 percent and high blood pressure was the second biggest risk factor for cardiac disease in Grenada. This suggests that primary health care team skills and competencies should focus on lowering and maintaining normal blood pressure, as well as in eliciting patients' involvement in managing their disease (PAHO 2013).

Diabetes

YLLs due to diabetes increased 122 percent between 1990 and 2010. Diabetes was the fourth leading cause of YLDs and the second highest cause of DALYs. Dietary risks and high body mass index are two of Grenada's biggest risk factors for diabetes, which highlights the need to devote considerable attention to diabetes prevention; this requires primary care teams to develop a range of NCD prevention competencies, such as behavior change counseling (PAHO 2013).

Gap Analysis for HRH Planning and Management to Combat NCDs

Grenada meets global targets for the competencies and coverage of primary care teams and public health skills. But it only meets the minimum targets, and its current staffing profile does not meet the requirements indicated by its current or predicted NCD profile.

The management of nurses is a particular concern: many do not show up for work, leave early, or take extended periods of medical leave (ranging from three months to one year). In addition to their 21 to 35 days of vacation a year, nurses are granted 20 days of sick leave. When they take leave, they are seldom replaced, which leads to shortages in hospitals and clinics. The rise in NCDs is also affecting the nursing staff. Grenada has a shortage of nurses with specialization training, including nurses trained in dialysis, oncology, psychiatry, family nurse practitioners, intensive care, geriatrics, and community health nursing.

Although Grenada is graduating more nurses than can be hired, many experienced nurses are reaching retirement age, raising concerns that there will be an experience gap once they retire. Many recent nurse graduates also find it difficult getting nursing jobs in Grenada. To compensate for the lack of in-country employment, the government has an arrangement with Trinidad and Tobago to absorb many new Grenadian nurse graduates.

Migration is so far not a major issue. However, with neighboring Trinidad and Tobago absorbing nurses from Grenada at better pay and benefits, this could draw nurses, particularly midwives, out of Grenada, resulting in a shortage of trained nurses.

Interviewees agreed that the quality of nurses has deteriorated over the years. Customer service is a particular concern: many patients complain about how nurses treat them, citing a lack of empathy, rudeness, and delays in starting procedures. This is an area that could be included in training to improve the quality of patient care. Some of the negative reaction may be explained by the conditions under which nurses work. Their pay is low for the region, opportunities for career advancement are limited, working hours are long, and the paperwork has increased.

The government has instituted a structural adjustment program imposing a hiring freeze for nurses in which no new positions can be created and no vacant positions can be filled.

Table A.8 outlines Grenada's HRH staffing profile for combatting NCDs.

Legislation Affecting HRH Planning

Table A.9 outlines the status of Grenada's legislation dealing with HRH planning. Legislation covering essential services, health, and safety is notably absent.

Other legislation relevant to HRH planning includes the following (Abt Associates 2012a):

- Grenada Constitution Act (1973)
- Employment Act (1999, 2000)
- Terms and Conditions of Employment Act (1968, 1990)
- Labour Relations Act (1999, 2000, 2003)

Table A.8   HRH Staffing Profile for Treating NCDs, Grenada

Number of HRH by key NCD professional category (2008)		
Professional category	Total (No.)	Density (per 10,000 population)
Doctors	69	7.6
Nurses and midwives	398	43.9
Rehabilitation specialists	5	0.6
Nutritionists	1	0.1
Doctors, nurses, midwives	467	51.5
All health care providers	632	69.7
All health workers	974	107.3
Number of staff in community health	180	
Number of medical specialists[a]	20	
Specialist type		
Cardiologists	0	
Rehabilitation specialists	0	
Neurologists	0	
Oncologists	0	
Pathologists	1	
Radiologists	1	
HRH targets related to the management of chronic NCDs (2011)		
Description	Target	Level of progress
HRH density per 10,000 population	25	100 percent (53)
Primary health care teams with broad range of skills	—	80 percent
Proportion of doctors in primary health care	40 percent	100 percent
Proportion of workers with primary health skills	70 percent	13 percent
Proportion of managers with primary health skills	60 percent	83 percent

Source: Information collected by the Pan American Health Organization from 2008 and 2012 as part of the Regional Goals for Human Resources for Health 2007–15 initiative.
Note: — = not available; HRH = human resources for health; NCD = noncommunicable disease.
a. Senior medical doctors by specialty: anesthesia (3); maxillofacial surgeon (1); physician specialist (2); surgeon specialist (2); gynecology (3); orthopedic surgery (2); pediatrics (2); ear, nose, throat (1); ophthalmology (1); pathology (1); radiology (1); psychiatrist (1).

- National Insurance Act (1983, latest amendment 2011)
- Foreign Nationals and Commonwealth Citizens (Employment) Act (1968, 1972, 1978, 2001)
- Caribbean Community Skilled Nationals Act (1995, 2006)
- Public Health Act (1973, 1981)
- Recruiting of Workers Act (1939)

Core Components for Strategic HRH Planning and Management

Grenada has started work on all four core components—a national health plan, an HRH management unit or function within the Ministry of Health, an HRH information system, and a multisector HRH taskforce—for strategic HRH planning and management.

Table A.9 Legislation Related to HRH Planning, Grenada

Legislation area	In place	Legislation and statutes
Legislation covering essential services	No	For essential services the Minister of Health can ensure that parties go to arbitration in accordance with the Labour Relations Act. However, there is no legislation covering essential services.
Legislation covering trade union formation and industrial relations	Yes	Labour Relations Act (1999, 2000, 2003) Labour Code Trade Union Act Industrial Relations Act
Legislation covering health and safety	No	
Legislation covering health professionals	Yes	Health Practitioners Act (2010) Nurses and Midwives Registration Act (2003) Pharmacy Act (1987, 1991, 1992, 1995) Opticians Registration Act (1955) Medical Officers Act (1903, 1966)

Source: National legislation and statutes, Grenada.
Note: HRH = human resources for health.

National Plan for Health—In Progress

Grenada does not have a national health plan or an HRH plan, both of which are essential components to guide the health sector and to inform HRH planning. Its permanent secretary has acknowledged that HRH is an important component of the health sector and wants to move forward with the development of an HRH plan. The Ministry of Health is working with PAHO to design a strategic plan for health and an HRH plan.

A human resources audit conducted in 2012 will serve as the basis for an HRH plan. While the audit is an important tool that can show current staffing levels, a strategic plan for health is essential to identify priorities for the health sector, and then to plan for HRH needs to support these priorities.

HRH Management Unit—Not in Place

The Ministry of Health does not have a formal human resources unit. Four administrative officers handle basic human resources duties, such as managing vacation time, but no one is responsible for strategic planning, retention policy, or recruitment. HRH is primarily handled by the Department of Public Administration, which conducted the human resources audit. The Public Service Commission responsible for hiring and firing.

Despite the absence of an HRH management unit, individuals within the Ministry of Health play an active role in improving HRH. For example, the ministry is attempting to address absenteeism among nurses, and is conducting a study on general nursing that looks at absenteeism that involves focus groups with nurses. The study data has been collected and is awaiting analysis to determine policies that can be put in place to reduce absenteeism.

HRH Information System—Not in Place

The Ministry of Health does not have an electronic health information system. All health information data, except epidemiological data, are stored as paper records. Personnel records are also paper files, making it impossible to search a database for personnel who have had a specific training or specialization. A SmartStream database is being used by the Public Service Commission, and it handles some human resources data.

HRH Multisector Taskforce—In Progress

Grenada started to establish an HRH taskforce, but this process is currently stalled.

Enhanced Components for HRH Planning

Table A.10 shows that none of the enhanced components for HRH planning are in place in Grenada, though the country has tried to develop an HRH plan. HRH leadership is lacking and no clear champion within the Ministry of Health has emerged to move this issue forward. Without a strategic plan for the ministry, there is no process for aligning HRH planning with the ministry's needs (see table A.11).

Core and Enhanced Components and Practices for HRH Management

Table A.11 shows numerous core components and practices for HRH management are in the process of being put in place.

Performance Management—In Progress

Annual and semiannual performance appraisals are conducted using a generic public service tool, which is likely to omit information on HRH-specific standards.

Table A.10 Status of Enhanced Components for Strategic HRH Planning, Grenada

Enhanced components for strategic HRH planning	Exist
HRH plan	No
HRH leadership	No
HRH champion within the Ministry of Health	No
Process for aligning HRH planning with Ministry of Health needs	No
Process for aligning training needs with Ministry of Health requirements	No
Mechanism for coordinating activities between the private and public health sectors	No
Mechanism for coordinating activities between the community organizations and public health sector	No
HRH development and training plan	No
Financial and service delivery plan that balances reasonably expected health care resources and commitments	
Human resources policies and procedures	In progress
Estimates of national health accounts	No

Note: HRH = human resources for health.

Table A.11 Status of Core Components and Practices for HRH Management, Grenada

HRH core components and practices	
Performance management system	In progress
Standardized and transparent process for recruitment	Yes
Opportunities for continuing professional development or in-service training	Yes
Process for monitoring retention	In progress
Process for succession planning	In progress
Process for evidence-based workforce planning	In progress
Enhanced	
Human resources manual or employee handbook with employee acknowledgement form	No
Process to ensure employee awareness of all policies and procedures	In progress
Review process to ensure policies and procedures are legally compliant	Unknown
Annual review of legislative policies and procedures with employees	No
Process in place to ensure adherence to all policies and practices	Unknown
Policies and procedures written to ensure employees have a clear understanding of the content?	Unknown
Employee satisfaction survey conducted	Yes

Note: HRH = human resources for development.

Recruitment Plan—In Place

For established posts, the Public Services Commission conducts all selections and appointments; it also determines the terms and conditions of employment for all staff based on a request from the Ministry of Health. Moreover, all posts must be approved by the Department of Planning and Administration. The ministry submits recommendations for hiring and is sometimes included in interviews for senior-level positions. Because the ministry is unable to make hiring decisions, long delays in filling new or vacant positions are common, which in health care can have life or death implications for patients. Stakeholders acknowledged that because staffing requests were typically made when the national budget was being prepared, the processing of these requests tended to be hurried and lacked supporting data. This, in turn, constrains the Department of Planning and Administration in its effort to determine a justification for staffing requests.

The Ministry of Health has the authority to hire ancillary staff and contract persons (including retired personnel) for posts that have been approved but not established. The ministry also has the authority to assign nurses. Other assignments are determined by the Public Service Commission. The ministry may move staff laterally, but any other staff shifts such as promotions are the commission's responsibility.

Continuing Professional Development and Training—In Place

Health professionals in Grenada have access to continuing education and in-service training in areas as diverse as disaster management, medical coding, maternal and child health, management of NCDs, water monitoring, and the management of patients undergoing dialysis. The Ministry of Health, PAHO, St. George's University, and various professional associations offer on-site and online training for professionals.

For doctors, clinical teaching takes place every Friday at St. George's General Hospital in conjunction with St. George's University. Nurses at the hospital have access to in-service training that covers clinical skills and topics including management and staff appraisals.

Monitoring Retention—In Progress

Minimal information is available on staff retention rates. Some data on reasons for leaving the Ministry of Health are in the HRM module of SmartStream administered by the Public Service Commission.

Succession Planning—In Progress

The National Strategic Plan for Health 2007–11 identified major cross-cutting HRH issues, including poor succession planning. The only reliable HRH data in Grenada are in SmartStream, which was set up to support salary processing rather than human resources management. However, the system is now tracking those close to retirement, as well as the number of people who have left and their reasons for leaving. The payroll system is administered by the Ministry of Finance; human resources management functions are managed by the Public Service Commission.

Workforce Planning—In Progress

No human resources unit or formal data collection processes or mechanisms are in place for workforce planning at the Ministry of Health. The Public Service Commission and the Department of Planning and Administration perform many personnel functions for the ministry. However, the first two of three key steps for HRH workforce planning have been initiated following a ministry human resources audit, and a USAID report (Hatt and others 2012) provides additional data on health service delivery needs. As part of the audit, recommendations were made for improving various aspects of HRH within the ministry, including rationalizing HRH needs by realigning some of the services and promoting multitasking, and showing that any increase in the staffing complement should be supported by empirical data and job analyses and subject to Department of Planning and Administration review. In hospitals, the actual use of services or the average occupancy should be a major factor for determining staffing levels and justifying any staff increases.

St. Lucia

Demographic Overview

St. Lucia is an upper middle-income country in the Eastern Caribbean (map A.3). St. Lucia's total land area is about 620 square kilometers; it has 158 kilometers of coastline and no land boundaries. St. Lucia has 11 administrative quarters

Map A.3 St. Lucia's 11 Quarters

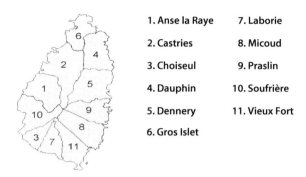

1. Anse la Raye	7. Laborie
2. Castries	8. Micoud
3. Choiseul	9. Praslin
4. Dauphin	10. Soufrière
5. Dennery	11. Vieux Fort
6. Gros Islet	

(17 electoral districts) (UNDP 2013). Even though it is an upper middle-income country, a 2005 poverty assessment found that 28.8 percent of the population lives in poverty.

According to St. Lucia's latest census in 2010, the estimated population is 173,720. The population rose sharply from 138,180 in 1990 to its 2010 level for an absolute population increase of 35,540 and a percentage increase of 20 percent. The population density (population per square kilometer) was 256.4 in 1990 and 329.1 in 2010, compared to the average population density in the Caribbean of 146.2 in 1990 and 177.6 in 2010 (UNDESA 2013). The United Nations Human Development Index ranks St. Lucia 83 out of 178 countries (UNDP 2013).

Health Care System

St. Lucia has launched several reforms to strengthen its health system aimed at decentralizing the country's service delivery model and emphasizing preventive care. Reform priorities included responding to the rise in NCDs by implementing universal health coverage, opening a new hospital, and converting two general hospitals to polyclinics.

The public health system, which is structured into eight health regions, provides primary care for 50 percent of the population and secondary care for 90 percent (MOH and PAHO 2011). Public health facilities include 33 wellness centers, two general hospitals, two district hospitals, one polyclinic, one mental wellness facility, one drug and alcohol rehabilitation facility, one home for the elderly, and one children's home. The health centers are well distributed throughout the country and offer primary health care consisting of medical and pharmaceutical services, maternal and child health, prevention and treatment of sexually transmitted infections, mental health clinics, cancer screening, dental care, nutrition, and the treatment of diabetes and hypertension (MOH and PAHO 2011). Most tertiary care, however, must be accessed in neighboring Barbados and Martinique. In 2014, the country opened a third general hospital

(New National Hospital) to expand access to care and alleviate congestion at the hospital level.

The private sector provides additional coverage, particularly for primary and secondary care services, through private physicians, medical centers, and a private hospital. Some nongovernment organizations also provide limited health care services, particularly in ocular health, disability, sexual and reproductive health, adolescent health, and chronic pain management.

Health Profile and NCD Burden

Life expectancy in St. Lucia rose from 68.9 years in 1990 to 73.7 years in 2010; health-adjusted life expectancy rose from 58.6 years in 1990 to 61.6 in 2010. The age-standardized mortality rate for all causes in 1990 was 891 per 100,000 population, falling to 722 per 100,000 in 2010. The largest reductions in mortality for all causes in this period were seen among the very young and older age groups; smaller reductions (and sometimes increases) were seen among young adults. Females ages 1–4 experienced the largest reduction in all-cause mortality (57 percent); females ages 80 and over saw the largest increase in mortality rate (12 percent) (UNDESA 2013).

For YLLs due to premature death, diabetes mellitus, cerebrovascular disease, and ischemic heart disease were the highest-ranking causes in 2010. Of the 25 most important causes of disease burden, as measured by DALYs, preterm birth complications showed the largest decrease, falling by 59 percent from 1990 to 2010. The leading risk factor is dietary risks (IHME 2013).

In 2010, the top five causes of premature death in St. Lucia were diabetes (2,100 YLLs, 7.2 percent of total YLLs); stroke (2,100 YLLs, 7.2 percent of total YLLs); ischemic heart disease (1,700 YLLs, 6.0 percent of total YLLs); preterm birth complications (1,500 YLLs, 5.3 percent of total YLLs); and interpersonal violence (1,300 YLLs, 4.4 percent of total YLLs). Changes in the leading five causes between 1990 and 2010 were diabetes (63 percent increase), stroke (27 percent decrease), ischemic heart disease (20 percent reduction), preterm birth complications (60 percent decrease), and interpersonal violence (179 percent increase) (IHME 2013).

Among the top 25 causes of premature mortality, 14 showed reductions and 5 showed increases of 25 percent or greater between 1990 and 2010. On the rise were diabetes (7.2 percent of total YLLs, 63 percent increase); interpersonal violence (4.4 percent of total YLLs, 179 percent increase); prostate cancer (1.6 percent of total YLLs, 39 percent increase); liver cancer (1.5 percent of total YLLs, 25 percent increase); and lung cancer (1.0 percent of total YLLs, 38 percent increase) (IHME 2013).

The top five leading causes of YLDs in St. Lucia are exposure to forces of nature, major depressive disorder, lower back pain, iron-deficiency anemia, and diabetes mellitus (IHME 2013).

The top three causes of DALYs in 2010 were diabetes mellitus, exposure to forces of nature, and cerebrovascular disease. Among the 10 leading causes of

DALYs in 2010 that were not present in 1990 were exposure to forces of nature, lower back pain, and interpersonal violence (IHME 2013).

Overall, the three risk factors that account for the greatest disease burden in St. Lucia are linked to nutrition—dietary risks, high body mass index, and high fasting plasma glucose. This, combined with St. Lucia's high diabetes burden, suggests that the country's seven nutritionists are not enough to cope with the problem, and that a nutritionist should be part of each primary health care team. Because diabetes is an uncontrolled health issue in the country, physicians skilled in dealing with the disease's complications will also be needed, such as diabetologists and nephrologists. The leading risk factors for children ages under five and adults ages 15–49 in 2010 were suboptimal breastfeeding and alcohol use, respectively (IHME 2013).

Of the four major NCD groups (cancer, cerebrovascular disease, cardiac disease, diabetes), three rank among the leading causes of premature mortality in St. Lucia. To cope with the burden of NCDs, the National Strategic Plan for Health 2006–11 proposed that the country's health system be restructured to further emphasize community-based prevention and primary care services, rather than managing chronic diseases through hospitals. The regional health teams proposed in the national strategic plan have yet to be put in place (Rodriguez and others 2012).

Cancer
YLLs due to prostate, liver, and lung cancer have increased significantly in the past 20 years (39 percent, 25 percent and 38 percent, respectively). In conducting workforce planning, it is worth considering incorporating medical specialists such as oncologists (and possibly urologists), along with relevant allied professionals, to provide palliative and rehabilitative care (PAHO 2013).

Cerebrovascular Disease
Between 1990 and 2010, YLLs due to stroke decreased by 27 percent, although it remains the second highest cause of premature mortality in the country. This suggests the need to strengthen capacity to diagnose and manage stroke in emergency settings and to raise awareness of stroke-onset symptoms, so that medical assistance can be provided as early as possible. Stroke was the third largest cause of DALYs in 2010, which suggests the need for improved rehabilitation services. It is unclear whether St. Lucia's 16 rehabilitation specialists are sufficient. Further monitoring of stroke outcome trends is needed (PAHO 2013).

Cardiac Disease
Between 1990 and 2010, YLLs due to ischemic heart disease declined 20 percent, although this was still the third leading cause of premature death in 2010.

Standards that define good heart disease care require staff who are able to rapidly diagnose and treat cardiac events (PAHO 2013).

Diabetes

YLLs due to diabetes increased 63 percent between 1990 and 2010, and this disease was the leading cause of premature death in 2010. Because diabetes is uncontrolled in St. Lucia, the number of amputees is growing, which could be contributing to diabetes mellitus's being the biggest cause of DALYs (PAHO 2013).

Influencing the control of diabetes among patients at the primary care level is a major challenge in St. Lucia, and because nurses are not formally trained to manage diabetes cases. A fee is charged at the primary health care level for conducting many NCD tests, which discourages patients from getting tested (Rodriguez and others 2012).

Gap Analysis for HRH Planning and Management to Combat NCDs

St. Lucia exceeds the minimum target for HRH density and has primary health care teams with a broad skill set. Although St. Lucia meets its target for the proportions of workers and managers with public health skills, the country still needs to increase the number of physicians in the primary health care system, and careful consideration must be given to the skill sets and competencies these additional physicians should have.

St. Lucia wants to increase the number of nurses (currently 500), particularly nurses with specialty training. A needs assessment determined that an additional 301 nurses are needed to deliver care according to the strategic health plan, including extra nursing staff for the New National Hospital and St. Jude Hospital. There are enough trained nurses to hire additional nurses, but much of the nursing pool is young and inexperienced. Budgetary constraints and an unofficial hiring freeze are the main obstacles to hiring more nurses.

Many of St. Lucia's nurses are nearing retirement, posing a significant age and experience gap when they leave. Because of their experience, retiring nurses are often the most qualified. To bridge the gap with newly qualified nurses, the country is hiring retired nurses on a short-term basis.

As in other countries in the region, St. Lucia lacks specialists, particularly nurses with training in intensive care, oncology, nephrology, pediatrics, and neonatal care. The country is also short of midwives. At present, 80 percent of specialty positions are filled by retired nurses. Since specialty training is not offered in country, nurses must travel abroad for additional training, but mobility from clinic to clinic is limited, and no direct incentives exist for obtaining specialty training.

The migration of nurses is not a concern right now. This has been a problem in the past for medical personnel in general, though not for primary care nurses.

St. Lucia's staffing profile does not match the requirements indicated by its current or predicted NCD profile (table A.12).

Table A.12 Staffing Profile for Treating NCDs, St. Lucia

Number of HRH by key NCD professional category (2008)		
Professional category	Total (No.)	Density (per 10,000 population)
Doctors	130	7.5
Nurses and midwives	329	19.0
Nurses, midwives, nursing assistants	371	21.4
Rehabilitation specialists	16	0.9
Nutritionists	7	0.4
Doctors, nurses, midwives	459	26.5
All health care providers	856	49.5
All health workers	1,485	85.8
Number of staff in community health	225	
Number of medical specialists[a]	48	
Specialist type	Number	
Cardiologists	1	
Rehabilitation specialists	0	
Neurologists	0	
Oncologists	0	
Pathologists	1	
Radiologists	1	
HRH targets related to chronic NCD management (2011)		
Description	Target	Level of progress
HRH density per 10,000 population	25	100 percent (41)
PHC teams with broad range of skills	—	97 percent
Proportion of doctors in primary health care	40 percent	30 percent
Proportion of workers with primary health skills	70 percent	100 percent (83 percent have primary health skills)
Proportion of managers with primary health skills	60 percent	100 percent (75 percent have primary health skills)

Source: Information from documents produced during 2008–12 including PAHO 2011.
Note: — = not available; HRH = human resources for health; NCD = noncommunicable disease; PHC = primary health care.
a. Full-time doctors at St. Lucia's two general hospitals by specialty: accident and emergency (12); anesthesia (4); gynecology (7); ophthalmology (2); pediatrics (5); pathology (1); radiology (1); general surgery (6); orthopedic surgery (2); ear, nose, throat (1); renal dialysis (1); cardiology (1); medicine (5).

Legislation Affecting HRH Planning

Table A.13 outlines the status of legislation that affects HRH planning in St. Lucia.

Other legislation relevant to HRH planning in St. Lucia includes the following (PAHO 2012; Rodriguez and others 2012):

- Public Health Act (1971, revised 2001) covers health care services, occupational health and safety, veterinary services, and health risk factors; and establishes the role of the Ministry of Health and its core function.
- Mental Health Act (1957) covers mental health care services.

Table A.13 Legislation Related to HRH Planning, St. Lucia

Legislation area	Exists	Legislation and statutes
Legislation covering essential services	Yes	Labour Act (2006). Section VIII (2) on regulation of disputes in essential services
Legislation covering trade union formation and industrial relations	Yes	Labour Act (2006). Section VII on trade union formation and operation; section VIII on industrial relations and disputes.
		Labour Code
		Trade Union Act
		Industrial Relations Act
Legislation covering health and safety	Yes	Labour Act (2006). Section IV on occupational safety and health.
Legislation covering registration of health professionals	Yes	Medical Practitioners Act (2009) covers doctors and dentists
		Nurses and Midwives Act (1993)
		Pharmacy Act (2000)

Source: National legislation and statutes, St. Lucia.
Note: HRH = human resources for health.

- Hospital Ordinance (1992) covers charges and fees for hospital services and establishing responsibility for payment.
- Family Nurse Practitioners Act (1993) authorizes family nurse practitioners to prescribe certain drugs.

Core Components for Strategic HRH Planning and Management

St. Lucia has two of the four core components of HRH planning and management in place—a national plan for health and an HRH information system.

It does not have an HRH policy, but the government hired a consultant on a six-month contract in 2014 to begin work on a human resources plan to address succession, retention, learning and development, performance, and leadership to align with the National Strategic Plan for Health 2006–11, which supports the delivery of primary health care. The human resources plan will also cover the private sector, with the aim of sharing data on private sector medical professionals to fill gaps in the public health system. This information will help the Ministry of Health engage private sector specialists when needed. St. Lucia's small population means that one specialist is sufficient to serve both sectors. Because no additional funds are available to cover the human resources plan, positions will have to be reallocated and repurposed without adding new staff or a human resources director.

National Plan for Health—In Place

In 2006, the government launched the National Strategic Plan for Health 2006–11. This outlines a vision of health reform and policy involving the Ministry of Health's role shifting away from health service delivery toward a stewardship role of coordination, regulation, and evaluation. By allowing greater managerial autonomy at the facility and regional levels, the ministry believes these services will improve, becoming more responsive to community needs and allowing ministry officials to spend more time on regulation and policy planning. The government is in the process of drafting a new strategic plan for health.

HRH Management Unit—In Progress

St. Lucia's Ministry of Health has no official human resources unit, although five administrative officers work on human resources personnel issues. The team, however, does not address strategic issues such as succession planning or retention.

The Ministry of Public Service handles hiring and firing. While the Ministry of Health may issue recommendations about hiring, the Public Service Commission has the final say. As part of public sector reforms, ministries generally are being given more control over the hiring and firing of their staff, but this transition has not yet been fully implemented.

Labor disputes are handled by the Public Service Commission and the Ministry of Labour. The Ministry of Health's HRH administration unit forwards labor issues to these agencies, though minor ones, such as those relating to working conditions, can be handled directly with the representing union, individual concerned, and within the ministry.

HRH Information System—Partially in Place

The Corporate Planning Unit has a comprehensive HRH database that details all HRH in public and private health care, but the Ministry of Health has no direct access to this database, though it can request information.

The ministry tracks the movement of staff, such as vacations and pending retirements, but has no central database tracking HRH skills, training, and education. Plans are under way to develop a single database to track all personnel information, including data from the human resources reports generated for the PAHO 20/20 report. At the department level, a paper-based system tracks where staff work.

HRH Multisector Taskforce—In Progress

In March 2014, St. Lucia set up its first HRH multisector taskforce. The National Human Resources Advisory Group includes representatives from the Ministry of Finance, Ministry of Public Service, Ministry of Education, Ministry of Health (including nurses and doctors), medical and pharmaceutical councils, and representatives from the St. Jude and Victoria hospitals. The development of a taskforce, which was part of the consultant's work on the country's HRH plan, will allow stakeholders to collaborate and form partnerships between the public and private sectors to meet HRH needs.

Enhanced Components for HRH Planning

Table A.14 outlines the status of the enhanced components for HRH planning in St. Lucia. As of writing, many of these enhanced components were not in place. However, the Ministry of Health is actively working on developing an HRH plan

Table A.14 Status of Enhanced Components for Strategic HRH Planning, St. Lucia

Enhanced components for strategic HRH planning	Exist
HRH plan	In progress
HRH leadership	Yes
HRH champion within Ministry of Health	Yes
Process for aligning HRH planning with Ministry of Health needs	Yes
Process for aligning training needs with Ministry of Health requirements	No
Mechanism for coordinating activities between the private and public health sectors	No
Mechanism for coordinating activities between the community organizations and public health sector	In progress[a]
HRH development and training plan	No
Financial and service delivery plan that balances reasonably expected health care resources and commitments	No
Human resources policies and procedures[b]	In progress
Estimates of national health accounts	No

Note: HRH = human resources for health.
a. Historically, the Ministry of Health has worked closely with civil society. Unfortunately, this active engagement has slowed in recent years.
b. The HRH unit develops Ministry of Health–specific policies and procedures.

and, with the help of an outside consultant, is putting the components in place to facilitate HRH planning.

Core and Enhanced Components and Practices for HRH Management

St. Lucia has two of the core components for HRH management in place—performance management system and opportunities for in-service training. The three other components—standardized processes for recruitment, monitoring retention, and workforce planning—are being developed. Table A.15 shows the status of the core and enhanced components for HRH management in St. Lucia.

Performance Management—In Place

As required by the Ministry of Public Service, staff appraisals are conducted twice a year. New nursing staff have a departmental orientation and a monthly evaluation by supervisors. The Ministry of Public Service is piloting a new performance appraisal system in four ministries, though the Ministry of Health is not one of them. The Ministry of Public Service is waiting for the system to be evaluated to see whether it can be shared more broadly.

Recruitment—In Progress

HRH was among the weakest components identified in the Eastern Caribbean's Evaluation of Essential Public Health Functions (PAHO 2008). The recruitment and deployment of HRH largely falls under the Ministry of Public Service and the Public Service Commission. The hiring of technical staff is a multistep process. First, the Ministry of Public Health determines the posts that are needed, which is subject to cabinet approval. Nurse supervisors at the regional level

Table A.15 Components and Practices for HRH Management, St. Lucia

Components and practices for HRH management	
Core	
Performance management system	Yes
Standardized and transparent recruitment process	In progress
Opportunities for continuing professional development or in-service training	Yes
Process for monitoring retention	In progress
Process for succession planning	No
Process for evidence-based workforce planning	In progress
Enhanced	
Human resources manual or employee handbook with employee acknowledgement form	No
Process to ensure employee awareness of all policies and procedures	No
Review process to ensure policies and procedures are legally compliant	No
Annual review of legislative policies and procedures with employees	No
Process in place to ensure adherence to all policies and practices	No
Policies and procedures written to ensure employees have a clear understanding of the content	No
Employee satisfaction survey conducted	No

Note: HRH = human resources for health.

discuss staffing needs with the chief nursing officer, who makes a request and justification for the hire to the permanent secretary. This request is sent to the Ministry of Public Service for review and approval; the Ministry of Finance allocates funds and the recruitment process itself is managed by the Public Service Commission. The Ministry of Health has some latitude in hiring administrative and ancillary staff, and its recommendations to the commission are generally accepted. The ministry can enter into temporary contracts with technical personnel for already approved posts, subject to the oversight of the Ministry of Public Service, and this is done regularly.

Continued Professional Development and Training—In Place
Some opportunities for in-service professional development exist, but it is difficult for staff to get released from duty to attend training because their absence would lead to staff shortages. St. Lucia does not have a training plan, but the combined challenge of a hiring freeze, inadequate numbers of technical staff, and the growing disease burden of NCDs supports the case for developing a comprehensive HRH training plan. The Ministry of Health is moving toward a fully integrated primary health care system, and this requires that staff receive training in crucial knowledge and skills. In addition to in-service training offered by the Ministry of Health, PAHO, and nongovernment organizations, medical and pharmacy councils offer continuing medical education training in partnership with provider associations.

Monitoring Retention Plan—In Progress
Retention of human resources in health is relatively stable, especially at the primary care level.

Succession Planning—Not in Place
Planning for the retirement of key medical personnel is necessary to maintain continuity in programming. This planning must ensure that new personnel are recruited, trained, and mentored to meet future needs. Although St. Lucia has no formal succession plan, department heads inform staff of needs and motivate them to pursue specialty training to address shortages. This is discussed during the biannual staff performance assessments.

Workforce Planning—In Progress
The deployment of HRH is regulated and managed by the Ministry of Public Service. St. Lucia recently experienced a shortage of HRH, particularly in nursing and specialist services, both at referral hospitals and community health services. In 2011, shortages were reported in radiology, pathology, orthopedics, and obstetrics and gynecology.

In 2010, St. Lucia completed a baseline assessment of HRH, and secured support from the Commonwealth Secretariat for workforce planning and policy development. The assessment concluded that staff numbers were inadequate, and that redeployment and modification of job descriptions should be undertaken.

St. Vincent and the Grenadines

Demographic Overview
St. Vincent and the Grenadines encompasses a group of 32 islands in the Eastern Caribbean (map A.4). The country has a land area of some 389 square kilometers. The largest island is St. Vincent, with the Grenadines (including the seven inhabited islands of Bequia, Canouan, Mayreau, Union Island, Mustique, Palm Island, and Petit St. Vincent) extending south. The country has six administrative parishes and 13 census districts. The United Nations Human Development Index ranks St. Vincent and the Grenadines 83 out of 178 countries (UNDP 2013).

The country's total population has been quite steady, rising from 107,509 in 1990 to 109,316 in 2010, for an absolute population increase of 1,807 and a

Map A.4 St. Vincent and the Grenadines

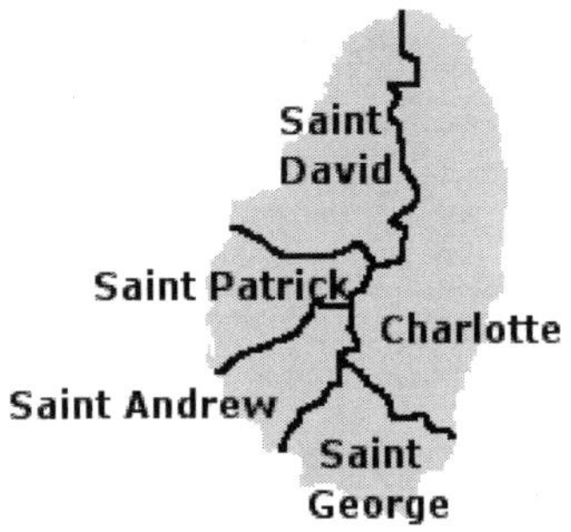

percentage increase of 1.7. The population density (population per square kilometer) was 277.1 in 1990 and 281.7 in 2010, compared to the average population density in the Caribbean of 146.2 in 1990 and 177.6 in 2010 (UNDESA 2013).

Health Care System

St. Vincent and the Grenadines has launched several reforms in recent years to restructure its health system to focus on primary care. The country reduced its health programs in an effort to model its health system on World Health Organization and PAHO recommendations for the structure of primary health care teams. Its chief medical officer used to oversee 15 programs and the permanent secretary used to oversee 3; this has been reduced to 3 and 2 programs, respectively. Human resources matters are the responsibility of the permanent secretary.

St. Vincent and the Grenadines is divided into 9 health districts; a reorganization, however, is under way to establish 11 districts. The country has 39 health centers, five rural hospitals, one main hospital, and one polyclinic. Primary and secondary care are available, but tertiary care must be accessed abroad.

Health Profile and NCD Burden

Life expectancy rose from 68.7 years in 1990 to 72.0 years in 2010; health-adjusted life expectancy rose from 58.5 years in 1990 to 60.2 in 2010. Age-standardized mortality rates for all causes was 890 deaths per 100,000 population in 1990, dropping to 753 in 2010. The largest reductions in mortality from all causes in that period was among the very young and older age groups, with smaller reductions (and sometimes increases) seen among young adults. The largest reductions in the mortality rate from all causes were among females ages 1–4 (49 percent). Males ages 30–34 experienced the largest mortality rate increases (11 percent) (UNDESA 2013).

For YLLs due to premature death, ischemic heart disease, preterm birth complications, and cerebrovascular disease were the main causes in St. Vincent and the Grenadines in 2010. Of the 25 most important causes of disease burden, as measured by DALYs, neonatal encephalopathy (birth asphyxia and birth trauma) showed the largest decrease, falling by 60 percent from 1990 to 2010. The leading risk factor in St. Vincent and the Grenadines is dietary risks (IHME 2013).

In 2010, the top five causes of premature death were ischemic heart disease (1,700 YLLs, 8.1 percent of total YLLs); preterm birth complications (1,300 YLLs, 6.3 percent of total YLLs); stroke (1,200 YLLs, 6.0 percent of total YLLs); diabetes (1,200 YLLs, 5.6 percent of total YLLs); and HIV/AIDS (1,100 YLLs, 5.4 percent of total YLLs). Changes in the 20 years since 1990 for the top five causes were ischemic heart disease (6 percent increase), preterm birth complications (54 percent reduction), stroke (27 percent reduction), diabetes (21 percent increase), and HIV/AIDS (90 percent increase) (IHME 2013).

Of the top 25 causes of premature mortality, 15 showed reductions and 6 showed increases of 25 percent or more between 1990 and 2010. Diseases on the increase were diabetes (5.6 percent of total YLLs, 25 percent increase); HIV/AIDS (5.4 percent of total YLLs, 90 percent increase); interpersonal violence (4.0 percent of YLLs, 101 percent increase); chronic kidney disease (1.6 percent of YLLs, 30 percent increase); cirrhosis (1.5 percent of YLLs, 25 percent increase); and prostate cancer (1.3 percent of YLLs, 63 percent increase) (IHME 2013).

The top five leading causes of YLDs in St. Vincent and the Grenadines are major depressive disorder, lower back pain, iron-deficiency anemia, diabetes mellitus, and neck pain (IHME 2013).

The leading three causes of DALYs in 2010 were ischemic heart disease, diabetes mellitus, and preterm birth complications. The 10 leading causes of DALYs in 2010 that were not present in 1990 were HIV/AIDS, lower back pain, and interpersonal violence.

Overall, the three risk factors that account for the most disease are dietary risks, high body mass index, and hypertension. In 2010, the leading risk factors for children ages under five and adults ages 15–49 were iron deficiency and alcohol use, respectively.

Of the four NCDs (cancer, cerebrovascular disease, cardiac disease, diabetes), three are the leading causes of premature mortality in St. Vincent and the Grenadines. Hypertension and diabetes accounted for nearly 70 percent of outpatient visits (Rodriguez and others 2012).

Cancer

Among malignant neoplasms, YLLs due to prostate cancer increased significantly— by 63 percent—over the last 20 years. Thus, including medical specialists such as oncologists (and possibly urologists) in workforce planning is worth considering (PAHO 2013).

Cerebrovascular Disease

YLLs due to stroke in St. Vincent and the Grenadines declined 27 percent between 1990 and 2010, although stroke remained the third highest cause of premature mortality. This reduction suggests the capacity to diagnose and manage stroke in an emergency setting may have been strengthened. But because stroke remains a significant cause of premature mortality more capacity is needed to reduce the amount of premature mortality and to focus on rehabilitation (PAHO 2013).

Cardiac Disease

YLLs increased 6 percent due to ischemic heart disease between 1990 and 2010, and this condition was the leading cause of premature death and DALYs in 2010. Good heart disease care requires staff members who are able to rapidly diagnose and treat cardiac events. Yet, St. Vincent and the Grenadines does not have a cardiologist. No data are available on primary health care nurses with cardiovascular disease management competencies (PAHO 2013).

Diabetes

Premature deaths due to diabetes increased 21 percent between 1990 and 2010, and this disease was the fourth leading cause of premature death in 2010. Diabetes was also the fourth largest cause of YLDs and the second largest cause of DALYs in 2010. Two of the three major lifestyle risk factors that contribute to most of the country's disease burden—dietary risks and high body mass index—are linked to nutrition, suggesting that the eight nutritionists currently on staff are not enough, and that this is a skill set that will need to be present in each primary health care team (PAHO 2013).

Gap Analysis for HRH Planning and Management to Combat NCDs

St. Vincent and the Grenadines has exceeded the minimum target for HRH density, though no data are available on primary health care teams and public health skills. The fact that the two leading risk factors are related to nutrition (dietary risks and high body mass index) highlights the need for behavioral change counseling and nutritional advice competencies within primary health care teams, as well as a need to provide access to nutrition and dietary services.

Although St. Vincent and the Grenadines has enough nurses, as do other countries in the region, it has a shortage of specialists, particularly family nurses, nurse practitioners, and nurses trained in diabetes care and emergency. Even though the rise in diabetes has led to an increase in amputations, no nurses in the country are trained in the rehabilitation of amputations; thus amputee patients are not being restored to their maximum function.

Since 2008, St. Vincent and the Grenadines increased the number of nurses it trains from 35 a year to 100; as a result, the country now has a surplus of trained nurses and plans to send some of them to work in other countries.

Migration is an issue and linked to low pay. This is particularly problematic in the loss of qualified nurses and specialists, who are recruited by other countries at better pay.

St. Vincent and the Grenadines' staffing profile does not meet the requirements indicated by its current or predicted NCD profile (table A.16).

Legislation Affecting HRH Planning

Table A.17 outlines the status of the country's key legislation that affects HRH planning. Legislation covering health and safety and essential services is noticeably absent.

Other related legislation in St. Vincent and the Grenadines includes the following (Rodriguez and others 2012):

- Public Health Act (1977) grants the Ministry of Health broad authority to regulate and enforce health codes in private businesses and homes, including food production and storage, water purification, and mosquito control.
- General Nursing Council Rules (1990) provide for councils to oversee the registration and practice of medicine, nursing, and pharmacy.

Table A.16 HRH Staffing Profile for Treating NCDs, St. Vincent and the Grenadines

Number of HRH by key NCD professional category (2008)		
Professional category	Total (No.)	Density (per 10,000 population)
Doctors	62	5.8
Nurses and midwives	268	25.2
Nurses, midwives, nursing assistants	208	19.6
Rehabilitation specialists	5	0.5
Nutritionists	8	0.8
Doctors, nurses, midwives	330	31.1
All health care providers	699	65.8
All health workers	923	86.9
Number of staff in community health	156	
Number of medical specialists[a]	13	
Specialist type		
Cardiologists	0	
Rehabilitation specialists	0	
Neurologists	0	
Oncologists	0	
Pathologists	1	
Radiologists	1	

HRH targets related to chronic NCD management (2008)		
Description	Target	Level of progress
HRH density (per 10,000 population)	25	100 percent
Primary health care teams with broad range of skills		
Proportion of doctors in primary health care	No data available	
Proportion of workers with primary health skills		
Proportion of managers with primary health skills		

Source: Information collected by the Pan American Health Organization from 2008 to 2012 as part of the Regional Goals for Human Resources for Health 2007–15 initiative.
Note: HRH = human resources for health; NCD = noncommunicable disease.
a. Senior medical doctors at the Milton Cato Memorial Hospital by specialty: anesthesia (1), internal medicine (2), gynecology (2), pediatrics (2), pathology (1), radiology (1), general surgery (2), orthopedic surgery (1), and urology (1).

Table A.17 Legislation Related to HRH Planning, St. Vincent and the Grenadines

Legislation area	Exists	Legislation and statutes
Legislation covering essential services	No	
Legislation covering trade union formation and industrial relations	Yes	Trade Union Act (1950, amended 1988)
		Trade Disputes Act (Arbitration and Inquiry) Act (1940, amended 1987)
		Trade Union Rules (1990)
		Labour Code
		Industrial Relations Act
Legislation covering health and safety	No	
Legislation covering health professionals	Yes	Medical Registration Act
		General Nursing Registration Act
		Pharmacy Act

Source: National legislation and statutes, St. Vincent and the Grenadines parishes.
Note: HRH = human resources for health; NCD = noncommunicable disease.

- Milton Cato Schedule of Fees (1995).
- Mental Health Act (1958, amended 1991) regulates the conditions under which patients may be voluntarily admitted to the Mental Health Rehabilitation Center.

Core Components for Strategic HRH Planning and Management

Of the four core components for strategic HRH planning and management, St. Vincent and the Grenadines has only one in place—a national plan for health.

The country has no HRH policy, and the handling of most HRH is unwritten. Ministry of Health officials acknowledge that an official human resources unit needs to be developed, and human resources need to be better managed and planned. Before developing an HRH policy, however, the ministry needs to look at the country's epidemiological profile and finish the strategic plan for the health sector to establish priority health areas.

National Plan for Health—In Progress

St. Vincent and the Grenadines is in the process of developing a strategic plan for health to replace the one that ended in 2012. With PAHO's help, the country hired a consultant to evaluate the previous plan and the results of this review will be used to develop a new one.

HRH Management Unit—Not in Place

St. Vincent and the Grenadines does not have a human resources planning or management function unit in the Ministry of Health. Administrative officers handle basic human resources functions, but no one is in charge of strategic human resources planning, including succession and retention planning.

The Public Service Commission makes most human resources decisions, including hiring and firing. The Ministry of Health reviews applicants and recommends candidates for positions, but it is not usually involved in the interviews. Consequently, those interviewing the candidates often do not have the technical background to properly ascertain the quality of the candidates.

HRH Information System—In Progress

HRH information is handled in conjunction with other ministries. SmartStream management software—which can manage finances, human resources, assets, and performance management—is being rolled out throughout the public sector. The software's characteristics have led the government to stagger its implementation across the health sector. The Service Commissions Department is currently using SmartStream to manage payroll for the entire public service. The government has bought the human resources module and plans to expand the use of SmartStream to include other human resources functions, such as education, experience, and time in post.

Human resources data tracked by the Ministry of Health is limited to a list of employees, leave requests, and employee stations. The ministry is looking at adding skills, qualifications, and distribution to this database, as well as the ability to run reports, so that information can be better used.

An electronic database system similar to other open-source systems used in the region is being rolled out in clinics to track data in nine areas, including clinical data, supply chain management, public health, finance, and patient transfer and discharge information. Coverage is estimated at 80 percent in all 39 clinics. The required software and computers are in place, but not all functions, and user uptake is limited. As a result, hospitals and clinics continue to rely primarily on paper records.

HRH Multisector Taskforce—Not in Place
A multisector HRH taskforce is not in place.

Enhanced Components for HRH Planning
As of writing, none of the enhanced components for HRH planning are in place.

Core and Enhanced Components and Practices for HRH Management
Most of the core components and practices are not in place for effective HRH management (table A.18).

Performance Management—In Progress
A formal performance management system is not in place, but will be implemented with the rollout of SmartStream management software. Supervisors initially assess nurses at intervals of three months, six months, and one year, and

Table A.18 Components and Practices for HRH Management, St. Vincent and the Grenadines

HRH management components and practices	
Core	
Performance management system	In progress
Standardized and transparent process for recruitment	No
Opportunities for continuing professional development or in-service training	Yes
Process for monitoring retention	No
Process for succession planning	No
Process for evidence-based workforce planning	No
Enhanced	
Human resources manual or employee handbook with employee acknowledgement form	No
Process to ensure employee awareness of all policies and procedures	Unknown
Review process to ensure policies and procedures are legally compliant	Unknown
Annual review of legislative policies and procedures with employees	Unknown
Process in place to ensure adherence to all policies and practices	Unknown
Policies and procedures written to ensure employees have a clear understanding of the content	Unknown
Employee satisfaction survey conducted	No

Note: HRH = human resources for health.

subsequently annually. Once hired, nurses receive one month of orientation and an employee manual outlining policies and procedures.

Recruitment Plan—Not in Place

The Ministry of Health has no formal recruitment plan. When an employee resigns, the ministry requires that all vacation time be used before a replacement can be hired. After that, it requests formal approval from the Ministry of Finance to fill the position, and the Service Commissions Department then advertises the post.

Continuing Professional Development and Training—In Place

Several short-term training opportunities bolster formal educational offerings in the country. In-service training for nurses is conducted by the medical director at Milton Cato Memorial Hospital every Wednesday. Training covers a range of topics, including clinical care and management skills. Lecturers from Trinity School of Medicine often lead these seminars. An annual symposium gives medical professionals an opportunity to hear from overseas experts. Additional short-term training is offered by PAHO and nongovernment organizations in coordination with the Ministry of Health.

Monitoring Retention—Not in Place

No mechanisms for monitoring or addressing retention issues are in place.

Succession Planning—Not in Place

No method or tool used systematically to forecast the demand for new and replacement HRH is in place.

Workforce Planning—In Progress

In the absence of a strategic HRH plan or a needs analysis, staffing patterns are largely historical, with percentage increases in budgets guiding the recruitment of new staff. Because human resources functions for the government are located within the Service Commissions Department, the Ministry of Health's role in human resources management is often limited to advising the department and guiding existing staff. HRH management and planning functions within the ministry are not in place, and these are split between the chief nursing officer, the chief medical officer, and the health planner.

Notes

1. Presentation by Dr. David Johnson, chief medical officer, Dominica, at a Health Results and Innovation Trust Fund south-south exchange in Buenos Aires, November 2013. Based on 2011 data.

2. Presentation by Dr. David Johnson, chief medical officer, Dominica, at a Health Results and Innovation Trust Fund south-south exchange in Buenos Aires, November 2013. Based on 2011 data.

3. Figure based on percentage of the population with raised fasting blood glucose and/or those diagnosed with diabetes.

4. Presentation by Dr. David Johnson, chief medical officer, Dominica, at a Health Results and Innovation Trust Fund south-south exchange in Buenos Aires, November 2013. Based on 2011 data.

5. The slight discrepancy in the numbers provided by Dominica's Ministry of Health in March 2014 and PAHO's figures, which are included in table A.3, is due to the fluctuation in staff over different points in time.

6. Interview with Lilia Casey, dean of the Faculty of Health Sciences, Dominica State College.

7. Interview with Dr. David Johnson, chief medical officer, Dominica, March 2014.

8. The health districts are St. Andrew's, St. David's, St. George's South and St. George's North, St. John's/St. Mark's, and St. Patrick's on the island of Grenada, plus the Carriacou and Petite Martinique districts.

9. Data provided by the Grenada Ministry of Health during March 2014 visit.

10. Data provided by the Grenada Ministry of Health during March 2014 visit.

11. Data provided by the Grenada Ministry of Health during March 2014 visit.

References

Abt Associates. 2012a. *Dominica Health Systems and Private Sector Assessment: Strengthening Health Outcomes through the Private Sector and Health Systems 20/20*. Bethesda, MD: Abt Associates.

———. 2012b. *Grenada Health Systems and Private Sector Assessment: Strengthening Health Outcomes through the Private Sector and Health Systems 20/20*. Bethesda, MD: Abt Associates.

Hatt, L., D. Altman, S. Chankova, C. Narcisse, D.-L. Peña, and others 2012. *Grenada Health Systems and Private Sector Assessment. Strengthening Health Outcomes through the Private Sector and Health Systems*. Bethesda, MD: Abt Associates.

IHME (Institute for Health Metrics and Evaluation). 2013. *The Global Burden of Disease: Generating Evidence, Guiding Policy*. Seattle, WA: IHME.

MOH (Ministry of Health) and PAHO (Pan American Health Organization). 2011. *Saint Lucia Country Report: Baseline Indicators of the Regional Goals for Human Resources in Health*. Washington, DC: PAHO.

PAHO (Pan American Health Organization). 2002. "The Essential Public Health Functions as a Strategy for Improving Overall Health Systems Performance: Trends and Challenges since the Public Health in the Americas Initiative, 2000–2007." Working Document, PAHO, Washington, DC.

———. 2011. *Handbook for Measurement and Monitoring: Indicators of the Regional Goals for Human Resources for Health: A Shared Commitment*. Washington, DC: PAHO.

———. 2012. *Health in the Americas*. Washington, DC: PAHO.

———. 2013. *Health Situation in the Americas. Basic Indicators 2013*. Washington, DC: PAHO. http://www.paho.org/saludenlasamericas/index.php?option=com_docman&task=doc_view&gid=231&Itemid=.

Rodriguez, M., B. O'Hanlon, A. Vogus, R. Feeley, C. Narcisse, and C. Jodi. 2012. *Saint Lucia Health Systems and Private Sector Assessment 2011*. Bethesda, MD: Abt Associates.

UNDESA (United Nations Department of Economic and Social Affairs), Population Division. 2013. *World Population Prospects: The 2012 Revision*. New York: UNDESA.

UNDP (United Nations Development Program). 2013. *Human Development Report 2013: The Rise of the South: Human Progress in a Diverse World*. New York: UNDP.

Resource Persons Interviewed for the Country Case Studies

List of Resource Persons

Table B.1 shows the individuals interviewed for this publication's four country case studies—Dominica, Grenada, St. Lucia, and St. Vincent and the Grenadines—during the period March 16–24, 2014.

Table B.1 Resource Persons Interviewed

Name	Title	Department/Organization
Dominica		
Dr. David Johnson	Chief Medical Officer	Ministry of Health
Caesarina Ferrol	Principal Nursing Officer	Ministry of Health
Esprit	Executive Officer, Personnel	Ministry of Health
Buton	Administrative Officer	Ministry of Health
Irma Edwards	Chief Personnel Officer	Ministry of National Security
Powell	Permanent Secretary	Ministry of Education
Irene Ducreay	Education Officer	Ministry of Education
Lilia Casey	Dean of the Faculty of Health Science	Dominica State College
Shirley Augustine	Country Program Specialist	Pan American Health Organization
Grenada		
Aaron Francois	Permanent Secretary	Ministry of Health
Priscilla Hopkin	Acting Chief Nursing Officer	Ministry of Health
Lydia Francis	Chief Community Health Nurse	Ministry of Health
Dr. George Mitchell	Chief Medical Officer	Ministry of Health
Juliana Mitchell	Senior Administrative Officer, Personnel	Ministry of Health
Camille St. Louis	Planning Officer	Ministry of Health
Ruth Rouse	Permanent Secretary	Ministry of Education and Human Resource Development
Patricia Felix	Deputy Chief Education Officer	Ministry of Education and Human Resource Development

table continues next page

Table B.1 Resource Persons Interviewed *(continued)*

Name	Title	Department/Organization
Andrew Augustine	Senior Human Resource Development Officer	Ministry of Education and Human Resource Development
Tessa Stroudet	Country Program Specialist	Pan American Health Organization
St. Lucia		
Deborah Martial	Deputy Permanent Secretary	Ministry of Health
Anne Margaret Henry	Principal Nursing Officer (Community)	Ministry of Health
Marylene Paul	Chief Nursing Officer	Ministry of Health
Juliet Joseph	Assistant Principal Nursing Officer	Ministry of Health
Jacqueline Matthew	Planning Officer	Ministry of Health
Kerry Joseph	Health Planner	Ministry of Health
Jackie Joseph-Mills	Health Planner	Ministry of Health
Silka Tobias	Senior Human Resources Officer	Ministry of Health
Kelly Culver	Human Resources Expert	Commonwealth Secretariat
St. Vincent and the Grenadines		
Luis de Shong	Permanent Secretary	Ministry of Health
Dr. Simone Keizer Beache	Chief Medical Officer	Ministry of Health
Peggy Da Silva	Chief Nursing Officer	Ministry of Health
Ferosa Roache	Senior Nursing Officer, Community Nursing Service	Ministry of Health
Anneke Wilson	Country Program Specialist	Pan American Health Organization

Core Data Set for Developing a Human Resources for Health Information System

Background

This appendix presents a step-by-step plan for developing a human resources for health (HRH) information system. This is a core component of HRH planning and part of the toolkit developed for countries to strengthen HRH planning and management.

Data Characteristics

Data Quality

This project is based on high-quality data. Figure C.1 details the characteristics of quality data. If the quality of the data cannot be guaranteed, users should try to identify a secondary source to verify the data. At the start of data collection, it is anticipated that sources are regularly updated; electronic data (for example, payroll) will be the most reliable.

Data Levels

There are two data levels: (1) individual data, which are data made up of individual points, such as payroll and membership lists, and (2) summary/aggregate data, which summarize individual data, such as the total number of doctors registered with a medical council.

These levels of data can be electronic or hard copy (see figure C.2). For this project, individual-level electronic data (for example, payroll data) were tapped wherever possible; if that was not possible, electronic summary data were used. All electronic data should be transferred to an Excel spreadsheet. A later phase of this project will convert existing hard-copy information to an electronic format.

Figure C.1 Characteristics of Quality Data

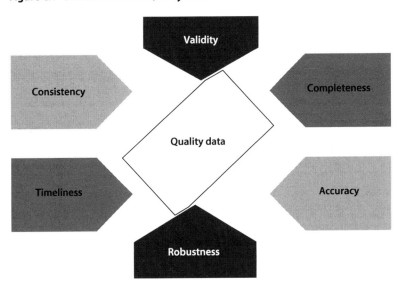

Figure C.2 Data Levels and Formats

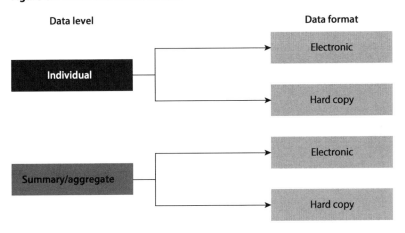

Potential Data Sources

A range of institutions and departments is involved in the production and management of HRH, and this is reflected in the range of data sources that need to be approached for this phase of data collection. A formatted spreadsheet has also been provided where it is anticipated that data will be held electronically. Table C.1 details the potential data sources for HRH data,

Table C.1 Potential Human Resources for Health Data Sources

Data source	Information to be collected
Payroll, hospital	Details of public health professionals
	See "Template for Electronic Data Collection"
Payroll, ministry of health	Details of public health professionals
	See "Template for Electronic Data Collection"
Ministry of health	Details of all ministry of health institutions
	Population by health district
	Total ministry of health workforce
	Number of vacant ministry of health posts
Registration councils or fees paid to registrar's/ treasury office	Number of private health professionals
	Number of public health professionals
	Registration status
	Qualifications
	Specialism
	In-service training
Professional associations	Number of private health professionals
	Number of public health professionals
	Registration status
	Qualifications
	Specialism
	In-service training
Yellow pages	Number of private health professionals
Statistics service	Population by sex and district (for example, parish)
	Total country workforce

together with information sought from each source. These sources will enable data to be collected on both private and public health sectors as well as on the education sector.

Data Collection

This section is a guide to facilitate the complete collection of the core data set. It is not, however, meant to be used on its own. This document should form the basis of weekly teleconferences and act to track progress during data collection.

Information will need to be obtained from a range of organizations and departments in both the public and the private health care sectors, as well as in relevant nongovernment organizations. This document is divided into the following sections:

1. Data collection preparation: provides details of the stages of the data collection process.
2. Data collection: forms and associated instructions to ensure complete data collection.
3. Data collection forms.

Data Collection Preparation

The following steps should be taken for the preparation of data collection:

1. Identify potential data sources for each professional type by completing form 1 (table C.2).
2. Complete column 1 by adding country-specific professional subtypes (for example, "gerontologist" under "Physicians").
3. For each professional group, complete columns 2 and 3.
4. For each professional subtype, complete columns 4 and 5.

Data Collection

This process involves four steps:

1. Request the following data from all the sources listed in the previous section: (a) head count; (b) sex; (c) age and date of birth; (d) location of work (health region/geographical subunit, urban versus rural, hospital versus nonhospital; and (e) private sector, public sector, or both.
2. Submit a formal written request for this information.
3. Contact the data source to confirm receipt.
4. Meet data source to obtain data and complete the appropriate table. Data collection tables are specific for each type of data source, so they will need to

Table C.2 Form 1: Potential Data Sources for Data Concerning Each Professional Type and Subtype

Column 1	Column 2	Column 3	Column 4	Column 5
Professional category	Name of registration council	Professional association	Name of private sector health care organization and department	Name of public sector health care organization and department
Physicians				
Nurses				
Midwives				
Dentists				
Pharmacists				
Rehabilitation workers				
Nutritionists/dieticians				
Community health workers				
Technologists (for example, radiographers, emergency medical technicians)				
Public health officers				
Laboratory health workers				
Health management plus support workers				
Other health workers				

be duplicated for each data source in that type (for example, the registration council table should be completed for all HRH registration councils, such as the general nursing council and the medical council).

Steps 2 and 3 can be omitted if a good relationship with a particular data source already exists.

Form 1 (table C.2) should be used to develop a comprehensive list of potential data sources for each health professional category. Each professional group will have up to five data sources (columns 1–5); noncore professional types have shaded gray boxes.

Data Collection Forms

Table C.3 is a data collection form for ministries of health and health authorities. If it is possible to obtain electronic data, they should send the data source in form 2, "Template for Electronic Data Collection" (table C.4).

Table C.3 Form 2: Data Collection Form for Ministries of Health and Health Authorities

	Ministry of health payroll or human resources office				
	Please input data in the space provided				
1	Total number of individuals in each of the professional categories listed		2	Number of primary health care (PHC) workers in district hospitals	
1a	Physicians		3	Number of PHC workers in medical centers	
1b	Nurses		4	Total number of PHC workers	
1c	Midwives		5	Total number of contract workers in the health sector	
1d	Dentists		6	Number of managers in health sector	
1e	Pharmacists		7	Number of physicians in primary care	
1f	Rehabilitation workers		8	Number of physicians at tertiary/secondary hospitals	
1g	Nutritionists/dieticians		9	Specialties of senior physicians at tertiary/secondary hospitals	
1h	Community health workers		COMMENTS		
1i	Technologists (for example, radiographers, emergency medical technicians)				
1j	Public health officers				
1k	Laboratory health workers				
1l	Health management plus support workers				
1m	Other health workers				

Ministry of health planning		
1	Population by health district	COMMENTS
	Name of district	Population	

Budget estimates			
1	Total of number of positions in health sector		COMMENTS
2	Total number of contract workers in the health		

Ministry of health/government training			
1	Details of in-service training courses		COMMENTS
2	Details of scholarships/study leave for postgraduate qualifications in noncommunicable diseases (NCD)/PHC		
3	Number of in-service training courses with PHC competencies		
4	Number of in-service training courses with NCD competencies		
5	Number of managers who have applied for study leave/ bursaries for management courses		

Community/primary health care services			
1	What percentage of the country's total population is covered by the PHC team?		COMMENTS
2	Which professional groups are included in the PHC teams?		
3	Is NCD management a competency required of the primary health care teams?		

	Board-controlled/national hospitals: payroll or human resources office					
	Please input data in the space provided					
1	Total number individuals in each of the professional categories listed in form 1, column 1		2	Total number of contract workers		
1a	Physicians		3	Total number of positions		
1b	Nurses		4	Number of vacant positions		
1c	Midwives		5	Number of managers		
1d	Dentists		6	Number of physician specialists		
1e	Pharmacists		7	Type of physician specialists:		
1f	Rehabilitation workers		7a	Oncologist		
1g	Nutritionists/dieticians		7b	Cardiologist		
1h	Community health workers		7c	Radiologist		
1i	Technologists (for example, radiographers, emergency medical technicians)		7d	Pathologist		
1j	Public health officers		7e	Rehabilitation specialist		
1k	Laboratory health workers		7f	Diabetologist		
1l	Health management plus support workers		7g	Endocrinologist		
1m	Other health workers			Please add any others		
	Training department					
1	Number of in-service training courses with/on primary health care competencies		COMMENTS			
2	Number of attendees in each course					
3	Number of in-service training courses with/on NCD competencies					
4	Number of attendees in each course					

	Census office			
1	Total population	2	Population by parish	
	COMMENTS		Parish	Population

The Nurse Workforce in the Eastern Caribbean • http://dx.doi.org/10.1596/978-1-4648-0830-2

	Registration councils (this section needs to be duplicated for each registration council)		
1	Total number of registered professionals		COMMENTS
1a	Number in private practice		
1b	Number in public practice		
1c	Number in both public and private practice		
	Any specialties		

	Professional associations (this section needs to be duplicated for each professional association)		
1	Number of in-service training courses with/on primary health care competencies		COMMENTS
2	Number of attendees in each course		
3	Number of in-service training courses with/on NCD competencies		
4	Number of attendees in each course		

	Yellow pages (alternative source for private practitioners)		
1	Total number individuals in each of the professional categories listed		COMMENTS
1a	Physicians		
1b	Nurses		
1c	Midwives		
1d	Dentists		
1e	Pharmacists		
1f	Rehabilitation workers		
1g	Nutritionists/dieticians		
1h	Community health workers		

Table C.4 Form 3: Template for Electronic Data Collection

Unique individual identifier	Employer/ organization ID	Employer/ organization name	Position name	Position ID	Job title	Location of post	Date of birth	Age	Sex	Are they also working in private practice?
1										
2										
3										
4 and so on										

Terms of Reference Template and Discussion Outline for a Human Resources for Health Multisector Taskforce

Introduction

This section presents a terms of reference template and discussion outline for creating a human resources for health (HRH) multisector taskforce, which is a core component of HRH planning. The template was developed as part of a toolkit for Eastern Caribbean countries to use to improve HRH planning and management.

Draft Terms of Reference for an HRH Taskforce

Background

The purpose of the HRH taskforce is to oversee, guide, and advise on the development and implementation of a strategic plan for human resources for health. This draft template can be used in conjunction with the discussion document to ensure that all aspects of the terms of reference are considered and addressed.

Purpose

The objectives of the multisector taskforce are the following:

- Identify emerging HRH issues.
- Develop recommendations for policy and decision makers.
- Provide a multidisciplinary forum for discussing HRH and related issues.
- Report annually to policy makers and stakeholders on the status of HRH.

Role
Structure and Composition
1. Structure
2. Membership

Principles of Operation
1. Logistics
   a. Meeting schedule
   b. Location
2. Decision making
3. Communication
4. Membership rules

HRH Taskforce Terms of Reference Discussion Points

Purpose
This document is to be used to promote discussion when planning the HRH taskforce and developing its terms of reference. The "Terms of Reference Template" can be used as a guide to ensure all aspects of the terms of reference are present and ratified.

Role
The HRH taskforce's role is to lead, coordinate, and provide oversight for all HRH strengthening activities and to manage the following activities on an initial basis:

- Establish consensus on the mission and purpose of the HRH taskforce.
- Agree on operating principles and terms of reference for organizing the HRH taskforce.

On an ongoing basis, the taskforce's role covers the following activities:

- Develop policy and management questions to inform data needs and Human Resources Information Systems (HRIS) functions.
- Define indicators to monitor the status of the health workforce via the HRIS.
- Identify existing information systems, including infrastructure, databases, forms, and collection mechanisms at all levels.
- Review reports that have implications for HRH planning.
- Assist the ministry of health to establish a framework for the development of human resources indicators.
- Provide guidance to the ministry of health for developing a human resources plan.
- Provide guidance to the ministry of health for identifying training needs.
- Share findings and tools with other ministries, sectors, countries, and regions.

Structure and Composition

Structure

- To whom is the HRH taskforce accountable?
- Who is the chairperson of the taskforce?
- Who is the secretary?
- Are there any other roles that need to be established?
- Are there any critical participants without whom the meetings cannot take place?
- Are there any smaller working groups within the HRH taskforce?
  - Education and training
  - Governance
  - Data and information systems
  - Partnerships and communications

Membership

This is not a prescriptive list and membership does not need to be limited to those identified here (when other key individuals are identified, they should be added to the list):

- Representatives from the ministry of education for data on scholarships, and so on.
- Representatives from training colleges, including community colleges and the University of the West Indies.
- One or two representatives from councils that work with licensing and regulations.
- Representatives from professional associations.
- Someone responsible for a payroll database.
- Someone responsible for an HRH database (if one exists).
- Representatives from the planning and analysis unit in the ministry of health.
- Representatives from civil service, public administration, information technology, and ministry of finance for data pertaining to HRH governance structures.
- Hospital staff, including a database administrator, the head of human resources, and the head of in-service training for all relevant professions.
- Representative designated by the ministry of health focal points.

Questions to consider include the following:

- Are all necessary groups represented in the taskforce or group, including internal and external stakeholders?
- When and how often will meetings be held?
- Where will meetings be held?

Principles of Operation

This section suggests principles of operation for the group or taskforce to discuss and agree on. This document will define the specific ways in which the group functions and the values that underline its operations. The final document will provide a reference for the group and ensure that expectations are clearly defined.

Logistics
- Agree on meeting schedule and location
- Define what constitutes a quorum

Decision Making
- How will decisions be made? By consensus, by majority rule?
- Is the group made up of primary and secondary stakeholders, or are all members of the SLG group equal?
- How are agendas decided? For example, matters arising from previous meetings and new items on the priority list of issues.
- How is activity and action point ownership determined?

Communication
- What documentation will be produced in these meetings?
- Who will produce and maintain the documentation?
- How will the documentation be distributed?

Membership Rules
- Can others attend or join the taskforce or group meetings?
- What attendance record is acceptable?
- Are all members expected to act as resources for one another?

Toolkit to Support Evidence-Based Practice

Background

Health services face significant challenges. As populations increase and life expectancy improves, the demand for health care outstrips the staffing and financial resources available (WHO 2002). Consequently, health services need to be improved by increasing efficiency and the quality of care, enabling limited resources to be used more effectively.

The Institute of Medicine recommends the following core domains for competency that are relevant to all human resources for health (HRH):

- Patient-centered care
- Interdisciplinary teams
- Evidence-based practice
- Quality improvement
- Informatics

This toolkit focuses on prioritizing and assessing competencies pertaining to evidence-based practice.

Definitions

Human resources for health. The World Health Organization's definition includes all people engaged in actions in which the primary intent is to enhance health. These include public and private sector nurses, doctors, midwives, and pharmacists, as well as technicians and other paraprofessionals.

Competencies. These are the habitual and judicious use of communication, knowledge, technical skills, clinical reasoning, emotions, values, and reflection in daily practice (Epstein and Hundert 2002).

Evidence-based practice (EBP). This involves making clinical decisions informed by the most relevant and valid evidence available. EBP has been described as the integration of clinical expertise and patient values with the best available research evidence (Sackett and others 2000).

EBP Competencies

The concept of EBP refers to the integration of the best research evidence, clinical expertise, and patient values in making decisions about the care of individual patients (IOM 2003).

EBP comprises five steps that form the basis for both clinical practice and teaching EBP (Dawes and others 2005):

- Translation of uncertainty to an answerable question
- Systematic retrieval of the best evidence available
- Critical appraisal of evidence for validity, clinical relevance, and applicability
- Application of results in practice
- Evaluation of performance.

These steps have associated skills (see table E.1); without these skills, health care professionals will find it difficult to provide best practices.

For EBP, two key documents were used to create the lists of competencies detailed in table E.1: the Institute of Medicine's *Health Professions Education: A Bridge to Quality* (IOM 2003) and the Sicily Statement (Dawes and others 2005).

Table E.1 Competencies and Skills for Evidence-Based Practice

Competencies	Skills
Know where and how to find the best possible sources of evidence.	Translation of uncertainty to an answerable question Skill: Knowledge to construct a question using the PICO mnemonic
Formulate clear clinical questions.	Systematic retrieval of best evidence available Skill: The ability to acquire and apply literature-searching skills across a variety of databases
Search for the relevant answers to those questions from the best possible sources of evidence, including those that evaluate or appraise the evidence for its validity and usefulness with respect to a particular patient or population.	Critical appraisal of evidence for validity, clinical relevance, and applicability Skill: A certain level of expertise in epidemiology and biostatistics Application of results in practice Skill: The ability to synthesize and communicate the results to relevant parties
Determine when and how to integrate these new findings into practice.	Evaluation of performance Skill: Requires the health professional to evaluate the evidence-based-practice process, and assess its impact within the clinical context in which it was implemented

Sources: Dawes and others 2005; IOM 2003; Rosenberg and Donald 1995.
Note: PICO = Patient, Population, or Problem + Intervention, Prognostic Factor, or Exposure + Comparison or Intervention + Outcome.

The Sicily Statement proposes the following to clarify and promote the realization of EBP (Dawes and others 2005):

- A clear statement of what EBP means
- A description of the minimum skill set required to practice in an evidence-based way
- A curriculum that outlines the minimum standard educational requirements for training health professionals in EBP.

Questionnaires

Having reviewed the competencies in table E.1 and having decided that EBP is a domain in which to build capacity, use the questionnaires in this section to assess departmental readiness and individual-level perceptions and attitudes toward EBP. To facilitate open responses to individual-level questions, the questionnaires can be completed anonymously and the results pooled to get a broad understanding of staff training needs. The results of these surveys will help in conducting competency needs and sensitization assessments, which can then be reviewed in light of the identified priority competencies.

This pack contains a Knowledge, Attitudes, Access, and Confidence Evaluation (KACE) for individual-level assessment, and an evidence-based practice questionnaire.

KACE for Individual-Level Assessment

The purpose of this survey is to measure students' knowledge and perceptions about EBP and critical appraisal skills. The EBP KACE measures knowledge, attitudes, methods for assessing evidence, and confidence in critical appraisal skills. We are interested in how your responses to KACE change as you progress through nursing school, and you may be requested to complete this survey again in the future.

To allow faculty to track your responses across more than one administration of the KACE, we are requesting that you provide your nursing school student number on the survey form. To protect your confidentiality, a research assistant with no involvement in this course or any aspect of the nursing school curriculum will create a randomly generated code number to replace your student number. The research assistant will not have access to a roster of names associated with student identification numbers. The randomly generated code number will be used to enter your responses into a data file, and your student ID number will be discarded. Your responses to the KACE will have no bearing on your academic performance in nursing school in any way, and your individual responses will not be known to the faculty members for this course.

The KACE has four sections:

- Knowledge of critical appraisal
- Attitudes about EBP
- Confidence in critical appraisal skills
- Accessing evidence

Knowledge of Critical Appraisal

Select the single best response for each question. We are interested in what you currently know. Please do not guess. Circle "Don't know" if that is the most appropriate response.

1. Published reports on treatments can be ranked on the strength of the evidence. Which one of the following is the most correct statement with respect to ranking of evidence?
   a. Clinical case studies are ranked higher than randomized controlled trials.
   b. Expert opinion is the lowest level of evidence.
   c. Laboratory animal research is the highest level of evidence.
   d. Research supported by national institutes of health is the highest level of evidence.
   e. Don't know

2. In judging the quality of the literature, which one of the following is the highest level of evidence?
   a. Article on a nonrandomized clinical trial that include references
   b. Case series article that has been peer reviewed and published in the *Journal of Medical Research*
   c. Cochrane Review of an oral health topic
   d. Detailed report of a clinical case by a recognized medical expert
   e. Don't know

3. If you were conducting a PubMed search to answer a clinical question pertaining to a patient, which one of the following would be the least productive search strategy?
   a. Limit search to current year.
   b. Limit search to specified type of article.
   c. Limit search using clinical queries.
   d. Search using appropriate MeSH terms.
   e. Don't know

4. Which statement is the most accurate on the number of subjects in a clinical trial?
   a. A power analysis should be conducted after the data are collected to assess whether sufficient numbers of subjects were enrolled in the study.
   b. If data are obtained from a large sample, an investigator can be confident that findings are clinically meaningful.
   c. Only large treatment effects can be observed when very large numbers of subjects are enrolled.
   d. Too few subjects may not allow true treatment effects to be seen when they in fact exist.
   e. Don't know

5. Which of the following statements best describes PICO?
   a. Checklist of guidelines to assist investigators with the reporting of the findings from a meta-analysis

b. Defines a specific MeSH heading and provides synonyms covered by that heading

c. Process for converting a clinical problem into questions that can be answered by searching for evidence

d. Technique for combining search terms to restrict a search to articles with specified elements

e. Don't know

6. A recently published study reports that patients with myofascial pain who received soft occlusal splints had less pain after two weeks than patients receiving a home physical therapy program consisting of jaw-movement exercises. Which one of the following factors could have contributed to this result?

a. Clinical examiners were blinded.

b. Patients in one group or the other did not adhere to treatment.

c. Patients were assigned to treatments randomly.

d. Too many patients were enrolled in the study.

e. Don't know

7. A statistical process that quantitatively pools the results of several research studies into one analysis is known as the following:

a. A Cochrane Review

b. A meta-analysis

c. Numbers needed to treat analysis

d. A systematic review

e. Don't know

8. Which of the following is the most appropriate study design to evaluate the efficacy of a new diagnostic device for assessment of oral health problems?

a. Blind comparison with a gold standard

b. Case-control study

c. Randomized clinical trial

d. Relative risk difference

e. Don't know

9. Which one of the following statements about test sensitivity and specificity is true?

a. Test sensitivity defines how many normal individuals the test will correctly identify as normal.

b. Normal individuals who have a positive rather than a negative result are classified as true-positives.

c. Sensitivity answers the question (if a patient has a positive test result, how likely is the patient to have the disease, and if the patient has a negative test, how likely is the patient not to have the disease).

d. Test specificity is the percentage of diseased individuals who have a positive test result as determined by a reference method or a gold standard procedure.

e. Don't know

10. Which one of the following statements about disease prevalence and incidence is true?
    a. Incidence refers to the percentage of geographic locations in a region where outbreaks of a certain disease are reported.
    b. Prevalence refers to the frequency of true-positive test results per 100,000 population within a one- year period of data collection.
    c. Incidence is the number of patients per 100,000 population who have a disease at a specific point in time.
    d. Prevalence is the number of patients per 100,000 population who have a disease at a specific point in time.
    e. Don't know

Attitudes about EBP

If you cannot respond because of lack of information, lack of experience, or uncertainty, please check the column in table E.2 labeled "uncertain."

Table E.2 Questionnaire on Attitudes about Evidence-Based Practice

	Strongly disagree	Disagree	Uncertain	Agree	Strongly agree
I believe that evidence-based practice (EBP) will be more valuable in my future practice than I did one year ago.					
I personally appreciate the advantages of practicing EBP care.					
EBP should be an integral part of the nursing school curriculum.					
I support EBP principles more than I did one year ago.					
EBP is a routine part of my professional growth as a nurse.					
The practice of evidence-based care has changed the way I learn.					
It has been difficult for me to practice EBP in the past year.					
EBP is a "cookbook" of clinical care that disregards clinical experience in providing the best treatment for patients.					
It is feasible to use EBP routinely when providing care for patients in the school clinic.					
EBP improves the quality of patient care.					

Accessing evidence

How frequently do you access clinical evidence from	Never	Rarely	Occasionally	Frequently	Very frequently
Colleagues?					
Textbooks?					
The Internet (excluding Cochrane Reviews)?					

table continues next page

Table E.2 Questionnaire on Attitudes about Evidence-Based Practice (continued)

How frequently do you access clinical evidence from	Never	Rarely	Occasionally	Frequently	Very frequently
Original research papers published in peer-reviewed journals?					
The Cochrane Database of Systematic Reviews?					
The Journal of Evidence-Based Medicine or subject-specific evidence-based journals?					
Continuing education courses/workshops?					
Podcasts and web conferences (webinars)?					
Databases of critically appraised topics?					
Confidence in critical appraisal skills					

How confident are you at appraising the following aspects of a published research report?	Not at all confident	Not confident	Moderately confident	Confident	Very confident
Appropriateness of the study design					
Bias in the study design or data analysis					
Adequacy of the sample size					
Generalizability of the findings					
Appropriate use of statistical tests					
Overall value of the research report					

EBP Questionnaire

Please answer the following questions about your background.

A. How do you best describe your agency/organization?
   - Central/Ministry of Health office
   - District health office
   - Local public health office
   - Other (please specify)
B. Although you may work in several capacities, which do you consider your primary position?
   - Health professional
     - District health officer
     - Health professional with management responsibilities
     - Health educator
     - Other (please specify)
C. On average, what percentage of your work relates to chronic disease prevention?
D. In what program area or areas do you specialize? Circle all that apply.
   - Diabetes
   - Obesity
     - Physical activity
     - Diet/nutrition
   - Cancer prevention and control
   - Tobacco

The Nurse Workforce in the Eastern Caribbean • http://dx.doi.org/10.1596/978-1-4648-0830-2

- Cardiovascular health
- Arthritis
- Asthma
- Infectious diseases
- School health
- Women's health, including maternal and child health
- Environmental health
- Healthy aging
- Other (please specify)

E. How long have you been in your current position?
- Years:
- Months:

F. Please indicate your gender.
- Male
- Female

Evidence-Based Decision Making

This set of questions asks about evidence-based decision making. For the purposes of this survey, evidence-based decision making involves the development, implementation, and evaluation of effective programs and policies in public health through the following:

- The systematic use of data and information systems
- The application of principles of scientific reasoning coupled with community engagement
- The appropriate use of behavioral science theory and program planning models

1. Based on your experience and best judgment, what percentage of all programs in your department are evidence based?
2. Based on your experience and best judgment, what percentage of all *chronic disease* programs in your department are evidence based?
3. What are some of the barriers to using evidence-based interventions or making evidence-based decisions that you have encountered?
4. In your opinion, what is the one thing that most needs to happen in your agency to increase the use of evidence-based decision making?
5. Please indicate the extent to which you agree or disagree with the following statement: I feel that I have the skills necessary for developing evidence-based chronic disease control. Use the scale to respond to each item by filling in the circle that best represents your response.

Strongly disagree										Strongly agree
0	1	2	3	4	5	6	7	8	9	10
○	○	○	○	○	○	○	○	○	○	○

6. Who expects you to use evidence-based decision making related to public health program planning? Please check all that apply.
   - Health department leader's direct supervisor
   - Coworkers
   - Community partners
   - Other (please specify)
7. Who expects you to use evidence-based decision making related to *chronic disease* program planning? Please check all that apply.
   - Health department leader's direct supervisor
   - Coworkers
   - Community partners
   - Other (please specify)

The following questions are on the use of incentives in your agency. An incentive refers to any organizational policy or practice that encourages the use of evidence-based decision making. Incentives may be tangible benefits, such as money or prizes, or intangible benefits, such as performance reviews, evaluation, support, or supervisory encouragement.

8. Which of the following incentives would most encourage you to utilize evidence-based decision making in your work? Please rank the top 2, where 1 is the most important.
   - Evidence-based decision making is given a high priority by leaders in my organization.
   - Positive feedback or encouragement
   - A performance evaluation that considers the use of evidence-based decision making
   - Training
   - Professional recognition
9. Are there any other incentives that would encourage you to utilize evidence-based decision making in your work? Please describe them:

Input from health care practitioners has led to the following definitions of skills needed to make evidence-based decisions to prevent chronic disease. Use the scale to respond to each item by filling in the circle that best represents your response. The rating on availability is specifically about how available you feel each skill is to you when you need it, either in your own skill set or in others.

10. What is needed to be able to prioritize health issues?

	Very unimportant					Very important					
	Unavailable					Available					
	0	1	2	3	4	5	6	7	8	9	10
Level of importance	O	O	O	O	O	O	O	O	O	O	O
Current level of availability	O	O	O	O	O	O	O	O	O	O	O

11. Quantitative evaluation (evaluation that uses data in numerical quantities, such as continuous measurements or counts): understand the value of quantitative approaches to chronic disease program evaluation.

| | Very unimportant | | | | | Very important | | | | |
| | Unavailable | | | | | Available | | | | |
	0	1	2	3	4	5	6	7	8	9	10
Level of importance	O	O	O	O	O	O	O	O	O	O	O
Current level of availability	O	O	O	O	O	O	O	O	O	O	O

12. Qualitative evaluation (this type of evaluation uses nonnumerical observations, using approved methods such as participant observation, group interviews, or focus groups): understand the importance of qualitative approaches to chronic disease program evaluation.

| | Very unimportant | | | | | Very important | | | | |
| | Unavailable | | | | | Available | | | | |
	0	1	2	3	4	5	6	7	8	9	10
Level of importance	O	O	O	O	O	O	O	O	O	O	O
Current level of availability	O	O	O	O	O	O	O	O	O	O	O

13. Developing an action plan for a program or policy: understand the importance of developing a chronic disease plan of action, which describes how the goals and objectives will be achieved, what resources are required, and how responsibility for achieving objectives will be assigned.

14. Translating evidence-based interventions: understand the importance of translating evidence-based interventions to prevent chronic disease in unique "real-world" settings.

| | Very unimportant | | | | | Very important | | | | |
| | Unavailable | | | | | Available | | | | |
	0	1	2	3	4	5	6	7	8	9	10
Level of importance	O	O	O	O	O	O	O	O	O	O	O
Current level of availability	O	O	O	O	O	O	O	O	O	O	O

15. Transmitting research to policy makers: understand the importance of using creative ways of transmitting what is known to work (evidence-based interventions for chronic disease prevention) to policy makers to gain interest, political support, or funding.

| | Very unimportant | | | | | Very important | | | | |
| | Unavailable | | | | | Available | | | | |
	0	1	2	3	4	5	6	7	8	9	10
Level of importance	O	O	O	O	O	O	O	O	O	O	O
Current level of availability	O	O	O	O	O	O	O	O	O	O	O

16. Making decisions based on economic evaluation: understand the importance of using economic data when making public health decisions related to chronic disease prevention.

	Very unimportant / Unavailable					Very important / Available					
	0	1	2	3	4	5	6	7	8	9	10
Level of importance	○	○	○	○	○	○	○	○	○	○	○
Current level of availability	○	○	○	○	○	○	○	○	○	○	○

17. Multidisciplinary partnerships: understand the importance of developing traditional and nontraditional partnerships to address chronic disease with evidence-based strategies.

	Very unimportant / Unavailable					Very important / Available					
	0	1	2	3	4	5	6	7	8	9	10
Level of importance	○	○	○	○	○	○	○	○	○	○	○
Current level of availability	○	○	○	○	○	○	○	○	○	○	○

The following questions are on the use of data in public health assessment, program planning, and evaluation. This refers to data sets like the Pan American Health Organization's STEPS.

18. Have you ever used public health data in your work?
- Yes
- No

19. I am confident in my ability to *find* public health data and statistics on chronic disease risk factors.

Strongly disagree										Strongly agree
0	1	2	3	4	5	6	7	8	9	10
○	○	○	○	○	○	○	○	○	○	○

20. I am confident in my ability to *use* data and statistics for public health program planning, grant writing, and community assessment.

Strongly disagree										Strongly agree
0	1	2	3	4	5	6	7	8	9	10

If the following resources were easily available to help with the adoption of evidence-based decision making, how likely would you be to use each of them? Use the scale to respond to each item by filling in the circle that best represents your response.

21. Policy briefs to provide information to policy makers about the importance of funding for evidence-based chronic disease control efforts

Least likely to use										Most likely to use
0	1	2	3	4	5	6	7	8	9	10
○	○	○	○	○	○	○	○	○	○	○

22. Targeted workshops that would address significant barriers to using evidence-based interventions (for example, economic evaluation, quantitative skills, translating evidence-based interventions)

Least likely to use								Most likely to use		
0	1	2	3	4	5	6	7	8	9	10
○	○	○	○	○	○	○	○	○	○	○

23. Individualized technical consultation that would address barriers to using evidence-based interventions (for example, one-on-one phone consultations)

Least likely to use								Most likely to use		
0	1	2	3	4	5	6	7	8	9	10
○	○	○	○	○	○	○	○	○	○	○

24. Distance training opportunities via webinar or video conference

Least likely to use								Most likely to use		
0	1	2	3	4	5	6	7	8	9	10
○	○	○	○	○	○	○	○	○	○	○

25. Distance training opportunities via conference call or CD-ROM

Least likely		Most likely to use			to use					
0	1	2	3	4	5	6	7	8	9	10
○	○	○	○	○	○	○	○	○	○	○

26. A peer-to-peer network where you could discuss issues and ideas with colleagues

Least likely to use								Most likely to use		
0	1	2	3	4	5	6	7	8	9	10
○	○	○	○	○	○	○	○	○	○	○

27. Are there other resources that you would find helpful in using evidence-based decision making? If so, what are they?

References

Dawes, M., W. Summerskill, P. Glasziou, A. Cartabellotta, J. Martin, and others. 2005. "Sicily Statement on Evidence-Based Practice." *BioMed Central Medical Education* 5: 1. doi:10.1186/1472-6920-5-1.

Epstein, R. M., and E. M. Hundert. 2002. "Defining and Assessing Professional Competence." *Journal of the American Medical Association* 287 (2): 226–35.

IOM (Institute of Medicine). 2003. *Health Professions Education: A Bridge to Quality.* Washington, DC: National Academies Press.

Rosenberg, W., and A. Donald. 1995. "Evidence Based Medicine: An Approach to Clinical Problem-Solving." *British Medical Journal* 310: 1122–26.

Sackett, D., S. Straus, W. Richardson, and W. R. H. Rosenberg. 2000. *Evidence-Based Medicine*. Edinburgh: Churchill Livingstone.

WHO (World Health Organization). 2002. *Innovative Care for Chronic Conditions. Building Blocks for Action*. Geneva: WHO.

Toolkit to Support Interprofessional Teamwork

Background

Health services face significant challenges. As populations increase and life expectancy improves, the demand for health care is outstripping available staffing and financial resources (WHO 2002). Consequently, the efficiency and quality of health care needs to improve, enabling limited resources to be used more effectively.

The Institute of Medicine recommends the following core domains for competency that are relevant to human resources for health (HRH):

- Patient-centered care
- Interdisciplinary teams
- Evidence-based practice
- Quality improvement
- Informatics

This toolkit focuses on prioritizing and assessing competencies pertaining to interprofessional team working.

Definitions

Human resources for health. The World Health Organization's definition includes all people engaged in actions whose primary intent is to enhance health. These include public and private sector nurses, doctors, midwives, and pharmacists, as well as technicians and other paraprofessionals.

Competencies. These are the habitual and judicious use of communication, knowledge, technical skills, clinical reasoning, emotions, values, and reflection in daily practice (Epstein and Hundert 2002).

Interprofessional team working. This refers to the levels of cooperation, coordination, and collaboration characterizing the relationships between professions in delivering patient-centered care (IEC 2011).

Interprofessional collaborative practice. As defined by the World Health Organization, this is "when multiple health workers from different professional backgrounds work together with patients, families, caregivers, and communities to deliver the highest quality of care" (WHO 2010).

Interprofessional Team Working Competencies

Interprofessional collaboration occurs when learners and practitioners; patients, clients, and families; and communities develop and maintain interprofessional working relationships that enable optimal health outcomes. Interdisciplinary teams have been shown to enhance quality and lower costs.

The documents used to create the domain and competency lists for interprofessional teams detailed in tables F.1 and F.2 were the Institute of Medicine's *Health Professions Education: A Bridge to Quality* (IOM 2003) and the Canadian Interprofessional Health Collaborative's *National Interprofessional Competency Framework* (CIHC 2010).

Table F.1 Interprofessional Team Working Competency Domains from Three Interprofessional Teams

Institute of Medicine	Interprofessional Education Collaborative	Canadian Interprofessional Health Collaborative
Ensure accurate and timely information reaches those who need it at the appropriate time. Customize care and manage smooth transitions across settings and over time, even when the team members are in entirely different physical locations. Coordinate and integrate care processes to ensure excellence, continuity, and reliability of the care provided.	Values/ethics for interprofessional practice: work with individuals of other professions to maintain a climate of mutual respect and shared values.	Patient-/client-/family-/community-centered care
Learn about other team members' expertise, background, knowledge, and values. Learn individual roles and processes required to work collaboratively.	Roles/responsibilities: use the knowledge of one's own role and those of other professions to appropriately assess and address the health care needs of the patients and populations served.	Role clarification
Communicate with other members of the team in a shared language, even when the members are in entirely different physical locations.	Interprofessional communication: communicate with patients, families, communities, and other health professionals in a responsive and responsible manner that supports a team approach to the maintenance of health and the treatment of disease.	Interprofessional communication
Demonstrate basic group skills, including communication, negotiation, delegation, time management, and assessment of group dynamics. Resolve conflicts with other members of the team.	Teams and teamwork: apply relationship-building values and the principles of team dynamics to perform effectively in different team roles to plan and deliver patient-/population-centered care that is safe, timely, efficient, effective, and equitable.	Team functioning, collaborative leadership, interprofessional conflict resolution

Sources: CIHC 2010; IEC 2011; IOM 2003.

Table F.2 Interprofessional Team Working Domains from Two Interprofessional Teams

Interprofessional Education Collaborative	*Canadian Interprofessional Health Collaborative*
Domain: Values and ethics for interprofessional practice	***Domain: Patient-/client-/family-/community-centered care***
Place the interests of patients and populations at the center of interprofessional health care delivery. Respect the dignity and privacy of patients while maintaining confidentiality in the delivery of team-based care. Embrace the cultural diversity and individual differences that characterize patients, populations, and the health care team. Respect the unique cultures, values, roles and responsibilities, and expertise of other health professionals. Work in cooperation with those who receive care, those who provide care, and others who contribute to or support the delivery of prevention and health services. Develop a trusting relationship with patients, families, and other team members. Demonstrate high standards of ethical conduct and quality of care in one's contributions to team-based care. Manage ethical dilemmas specific to interprofessional patient-/population-centered care situations. Act with honesty and integrity toward patients, families, and other team members. Maintain competence in one's own profession appropriate to scope of practice.	To support interprofessional collaborative practice that is patient/client/family-centered, learners/practitioners need to: • Support the participation of patients/clients and their families or community representatives as integral partners with those health care personnel providing their care or service • Plan, implement, and evaluate • Share information with patients/clients (or family and community) in a respectful manner and in such a way that is understandable, encourages discussion, and enhances participation in decision making • Ensure that appropriate education and support is provided by practitioners to patients/clients, family members, and others involved with their care or service • Listen respectfully to the expressed needs of all parties in shaping and delivering care or services
Domain: Roles and responsibilities	***Domain: Role clarification***
Communicate one's roles and responsibilities clearly to patients, families, and other professionals. Recognize one's limitations in skills, knowledge, and abilities. Engage diverse health care professionals who complement one's own professional expertise, as well as associated resources, to develop strategies to meet specific patient care needs. Explain the roles and responsibilities of other care providers and how the team works together to provide care. Use the full scope of knowledge, skills, and abilities of available health professionals and health care workers to provide care that is safe, timely, efficient, effective, and equitable. Communicate with team members to clarify each member's responsibility in executing components of a treatment plan or public health intervention. Forge interdependent relationships with other professions to improve care and advance learning. Engage in continuous professional and interprofessional development to enhance team performance. Use unique and complementary abilities of all members of the team to optimize patient care.	To support interprofessional collaborative practice, learners/practitioners demonstrate role clarification by: • Describing their own role and that of others • Recognizing and respecting the diversity of other health and social care roles, responsibilities, and competencies • Perform their own roles in a culturally respectful way • Communicating roles, knowledge, skills, and attitudes using appropriate language • Accessing others' skills and knowledge appropriately through consultation • Considering the roles of others in determining their own professional and interprofessional roles • Integrating competencies/roles seamlessly into models of service delivery
Domain: Interprofessional communication	***Domain: Interprofessional communication***
Choose effective communication tools and techniques, including information systems and communication technologies, to facilitate discussions and interactions that enhance team function.	To support interprofessional collaborative practice, learners/practitioners are able to do the following: • Establish team work communication principles. • Actively listen to other team members, including patients, clients, and families.

table continues next page

Table F.2 Interprofessional Team Working Domains from Two Interprofessional Teams *(continued)*

Interprofessional Education Collaborative	*Canadian Interprofessional Health Collaborative*
Organize and communicate information with patients, families, and health care team members in a form that is understandable, avoiding discipline-specific terminology where possible.	• Communicate to ensure common understanding of care decisions • Develop trusting relationships with patients/clients/families and other team members • Use information and communication technology effectively to improve interprofessional patient/client/community-centered care
Express one's knowledge and opinions to team members involved in patient care with confidence, clarity, and respect, working to ensure common understanding of information and treatment and care decisions.	
Listen actively and encourage the ideas and opinions of other team members.	
Give timely, sensitive, instructive feedback to others about their performance on the team, responding respectfully as a team member to feedback from others.	
Use respectful language appropriate for a given difficult situation, crucial conversation, or interprofessional conflict.	
Recognize how one's own uniqueness, including experience level, expertise, culture, power, and hierarchy within the health care team, contributes to effective communication, conflict resolution, and positive interprofessional working relationships.	
Communicate consistently the importance of teamwork in patient-centered and community-focused care.	

Domain: Teams and teamwork

Describe the process of team development and the roles and practices of effective teams.

Develop consensus on the ethical principles to guide all aspects of patient care and team work.

Engage other health professionals—appropriate to the specific care situation—in shared patient-centered problem solving.

Integrate the knowledge and experience of other professions—appropriate to the specific care situation—to inform care decisions, while respecting patient and community values and priorities/preferences for care.

Apply leadership practices that support collaborative practice and team effectiveness.

Engage oneself and others to constructively manage disagreements about values, roles, goals, and actions that arise among health care professionals and with patients and families.

Share accountability with other professions, patients, and communities for outcomes relevant to prevention and health care.

Reflect on individual and team performance for individual and team performance improvement.

Use process improvement strategies to increase the effectiveness of interprofessional teamwork and team-based care.

Use available evidence to inform effective teamwork and team-based practices.

Perform effectively on teams and in different team roles in a variety of settings.

Domain: Team functioning

To support interprofessional collaboration, learners/practitioners are able to do the following:
• Understand the process of team development.
• Develop a set of principles for working together that respects the ethical values of members.
• Facilitate discussions and interactions effectively among team members; participate and be respectful to all members.
• Participate in collaborative decision making.
• Regularly reflect on their functioning with team learners/practitioners and patients/clients/families.
• Establish and maintain effective and healthy working relationships with learners/practitioners, patients/clients, and families whether or not a formalized team exists
• Respect team ethics, including confidentiality, resource allocation, and professionalism

Domain: Collaborative leadership

To support interprofessional collaborative practice, learners/practitioners collaboratively determine who will provide group leadership in any given situation by supporting the following:
• Work with others to enable effective patient-client outcomes
• Advancement of interdependent working relationships among all participants
• Facilitation of effective team processes
• Facilitation of effective decision making

table continues next page

Table F.2 Interprofessional Team Working Domains from Two Interprofessional Teams *(continued)*

Interprofessional Education Collaborative	Canadian Interprofessional Health Collaborative
	• A conducive climate for collaborative practice among all participants • Cocreation of a climate for shared leadership • Application of collaborative decision-making principles • Integration of the principles of continuous quality improvement to work processes and outcomes
	Domain: Interprofessional conflict resolution
	To support interprofessional collaborative practice, team members consistently address conflict in a constructive manner by doing the following: • Valuing the potential positive nature of conflict • Recognizing the potential for conflict to occur and taking constructive steps to address it • Identifying common situations that are likely to lead to disagreements or conflicts, including role ambiguity, power gradients, and differences in goals • Knowing and understanding strategies to deal with conflict • Setting guidelines for addressing disagreements • Effectively working to address and resolve disagreements, including analyzing the causes of conflict and working to reach an acceptable solution • Establishing a safe environment in which to express diverse opinions, developing a level of consensus among those with differing views; allowing all members to feel their viewpoints have been heard no matter what the outcome

Sources: CIHC 2010; IEC 2011.

If you are not sure what interprofessional team working competencies your department or institution wants to focus on, use tables that were sent with this document. You can then use the questionnaires in appendix I to assess departmental readiness and individual-level attitudes and perceptions. The results of these surveys will help you to conduct a competency needs assessment, which can then be reviewed in light of the identified priority competencies.

Teamwork Perceptions and Team Structure Questionnaires

The questionnaire in table F.4 is based on the TeamSTEPPS teamwork perceptions questionnaire. Complete the questionnaire by placing a tick in the box that corresponds to your level of agreement, from "strongly agree" to "strongly disagree." Answer every question and select only one response for each question. The questionnaire is anonymous, so please do not put your name or any other identifying information on the questionnaire.

Table F.3 Structure: Teamwork Perceptions Questionnaire

Which of the following best describes your role?		
	Health professional	
	Health professional with management responsibilities	
	Administrator	
	Administrator with management responsibilities	
	Senior management	
	Senior management with clinical responsibilities	

Table F.4 Perceptions: Team Structure Questionnaire

Team structure	Strongly agree	Agree	Neither agree nor disagree	Disagree	Strongly disagree
The skills of staff overlap sufficiently so that work can be shared when necessary.					
Staff are held accountable for their actions.					
Staff within my unit share information that enables timely decision making by the direct patient care team.					
My unit makes efficient use of resources.					
Staff understand their roles and responsibilities.					
My unit has clearly articulated goals.					
My unit operates at a high level of efficiency.					
Leadership	Strongly agree	Agree	Neither agree nor disagree	Disagree	Strongly disagree
My manager considers staff input when making decisions about patient care.					
My manager provides opportunities to discuss the unit's performance after an event.					
My manager takes time to meet staff to develop a plan for patient care.					
My manager ensures that adequate resources are available.					
My manager resolves conflicts successfully.					
My manager models appropriate team behavior.					
My manager ensures that staff are aware of any situations or changes that may affect patient care.					
Situation monitoring	Strongly agree	Agree	Neither agree nor disagree	Disagree	Strongly disagree
Staff effectively anticipate each other's needs.					
Staff monitor each other's performances.					
Staff exchange relevant information as it becomes available.					
Staff continuously scan the environment for important information.					

table continues next page

Table F.4 Perceptions: Team Structure Questionnaire *(continued)*

Mutual support	Strongly agree	Agree	Neither agree nor disagree	Disagree	Strongly disagree
Staff share information regarding potential complications.					
Staff meets to reevaluate patient care goals when aspects of the situation have changed.					
Staff correct each other's mistakes to ensure procedures are followed properly.					
Staff assist fellow staff during high workload.					
Staff request assistance from fellow staff when they feel overwhelmed.					
Staff caution each other about potentially dangerous situations.					
Feedback between staff is delivered in a way that promotes positive interactions and future change.					
Staff advocate for patients even when their opinion conflicts with that of a senior member of the unit.					
When staff have a concern about patient safety, they challenge others until they are sure the concern has been heard.					
Staff resolve their conflicts when the conflicts have become personal.					
Communication	Strongly agree	Agree	Neither agree nor disagree	Disagree	Strongly disagree
Information on patient care is explained to patients and their families in lay terms.					
Staff relay relevant information in a timely manner.					
When communicating with patients, staff allow enough time for questions.					
Staff use common terminology when communicating with each other.					
Staff verbally verify information that they receive from one another.					
Staff follow a standardized method of sharing information when handing off patients.					
Staff seek information from all available sources.					

References

CIHC (Canadian Interprofessional Health Collaborative). 2010. *A National Interprofessional Competency Framework.* Vancouver: CIHC. http://www.cihc.ca/files /CIHC_IPCompetencies _Feb1210.pdf.

Epstein, R. M., and E. M. Hundert. 2002. "Defining and Assessing Professional Competence." *Journal of the American Medical Association* 287 (2): 226–35.

IEC (Interprofessional Education Collaborative). 2011. *Core Competencies for Interprofessional Collaborative Practice: Report of an Expert Panel.* Washington, DC: IEC.

IOM (Institute of Medicine). 2003. *Health Professions Education: A Bridge to Quality.* Washington, DC: National Academies Press.

WHO (World Health Organization). 2002. *Innovative Care for Chronic Conditions: Building Blocks for Action.* Geneva: WHO.

———. 2010. *Framework for Action on Interprofessional Education and Collaborative Practice.* Geneva: WHO.

Toolkit to Support Patient-Centered Care

Background

Health services are facing significant challenges. As populations increase and life expectancy improves, the demand for health care is outstripping the staffing and financial resources available (WHO 2002). Consequently, health care needs to improve efficiency and quality of care, enabling limited resources to be used more effectively.

The Institute of Medicine recommends the following core domains for competency that are relevant to all human resources for health (HRH):

- Patient-centered care
- Interdisciplinary teams
- Evidence-based practice
- Quality improvement
- Informatics

This toolkit focuses on prioritizing and assessing competencies pertaining to patient-centered care.

Definitions

Human resources for health. The World Health Organization's definition includes all people engaged in actions whose primary intent is to enhance health. These include public and private sector nurses, doctors, midwives, and pharmacists, as well as technicians and other paraprofessionals.

Competencies. These are the habitual and judicious use of communication, knowledge, technical skills, clinical reasoning, emotions, values, and reflection in daily practice (Epstein and Hudert 2002).

Patient-centered care. This is care organized around the patient. It is a model in which providers partner with patients and families to identify and satisfy the full range of patient needs and preferences. Not to be overlooked in defining patient-centered care is its concurrent focus on staff. To succeed, a patient-centered approach must also address the staff experience (Frampton and others 2008).

Patient-Centered Care Competencies

Many studies have shown that achieving patient-centered care can improve health status and other outcomes desired by patients. Complementary research has shown that patients who are involved in their care decisions and management have better outcomes, lower costs, and higher functional status than those who are not so involved (IOM 2003).

The competency lists for patient-centered care shown in table G.1 were created using the Institute of Medicine's *Health Professions Education: A Bridge to Quality* (IOM 2003) and the World Health Organization's *Preparing a Health Care Workforce for the 21st Century: The Challenge of Chronic Conditions* (WHO 2005). It should be noted that WHO's competencies are aimed at improving the care of chronic conditions.

Table G.1 Competency Domains for Patient-Centered Care

Institute of Medicine	World Health Organization
Share power and responsibility with patients and caregivers. This involves	
• Engaging in an ongoing dialogue with patients that brings about understanding, acceptance, cooperation, and identification of common goals and related care plans.	n.a.
• Guiding and supporting those providing care to patients by involving them as appropriate in decision making, supporting them as caregivers, making them welcome and comfortable in the care delivery setting, and recognizing their needs and contributions.	n.a.
• Understanding and respecting patients' self-management activities.	n.a.
• Providing physical comfort and emotional support.	n.a.
• Easing pain and suffering.	n.a.
• Providing timely, tailored, and expert management of symptoms.	n.a.
• Relieving fear and anxiety.	n.a.
Communicate with patients in a shared and fully open manner. This involves	Interviewing and communicating effectively
• Allowing patients access to their medical records.	n.a.
• Communicating accurately in a language that patients understand, and offering trustworthy information using patients' preferred communication channels.	n.a.
• Exploring patients' main reason for a visit, associated concerns, and need for information.	n.a.
Take into account patients' individuality, emotional needs, values, and life issues. This involves	Supporting self-management
• Providing care for patients in the context of the culture, health status, and health needs of the population of which each is a member.	Using a proactive approach
• Providing care that reflects the whole person.	n.a.

table continues next page

Table G.1 Competency Domains for Patient-Centered Care (continued)

Institute of Medicine	World Health Organization
Implement strategies for reaching those who do not present themselves for care, including care strategies that support the broader community. This involves accepting responsibility for enrolled members of a health plan, and considering the needs of underserved members of a community who do not initiate visits or present themselves for care.	n.a.
Enhance prevention and health promotion. This involves	Assisting changes in health-related behavior
• Applying population-based strategies to identify and reduce risk factors and to improve patients' use of and access to appropriate services and providers.	n.a.
• Defining and describing populations by health status.	n.a.
• Delivering health care services intended to prevent health problems or maintain health.	n.a.
• Understanding and applying principles of disease prevention and behavioral change appropriate for specific populations with which patients can identify; understanding the links among healthy lifestyles, prevention, and the cost of health care.	n.a.

Sources: IOM 2003; WHO 2005.
Note: n.a. = not applicable.

Review the patient-centered care competencies to determine if your department or institution wants to focus on this domain. If patient-centered care is a priority domain, you can use the questionnaires to assess departmental and individual-level experience and attitudes toward patient-centered care. Try to keep questionnaire results anonymous to facilitate complete and accurate responses.

The results of these surveys will help you to conduct a competency needs assessment, which can then be reviewed in light of the identified priority competencies.

This packet contains a departmental assessment tool created by the Picker Institute, and a patient experience questionnaire (Steine, Finset, and Laerum 2001).

If you are interested in comparing patient and physician perspectives, compare forms 1 and 2 (tables G.4 and G.5) for patients and form 3 (table G.6) for physicians.

Departmental Assessment Tool

Instructions:

1. Complete the table by marking the box in table G.2 that most appropriately captures the current status of the described practice in your organization.
2. Tally your score for each section, giving yourself 2 points for every practice that is fully implemented, 1 point for every practice that is partially implemented, and 0 point for every practice for which there is no activity or that is not applicable.
3. Calculate your organization's performance in each of the sections, and refer to the section of the guide addressing those areas in which your percentage performance indicates the greatest opportunities for improvement.

Table G.2 Snapshot of Implementation of Patient-Centered Care

	Fully implemented throughout the organization	Partially implemented (in progress or in place in some areas, but not all)	No activity	Not applicable
Setting the stage, strengthening the foundation				
The organization's commitment to patient-centered care is formally and consistently communicated with patients, families, staff, leadership, and medical staff (for example, mission and core values).				
Expectations for what staff can expect in a patient-centered environment are clearly stated and proactively shared.				
Patients and family members are invited to share their experiences with your hospital in focus groups.				
A patient and family advisory council meets regularly and actively provides input to hospital leadership on hospital operations.				
Patients and family members participate as members on hospital committees.				
The input provided by patients and families is used to guide the organization's strategic direction.				
Patient-centered behavior expectations are included in all job descriptions and performance evaluation tools.				
Staff at all levels, clinical and nonclinical, have the opportunity to voice their ideas and suggestions for improvement.				
Opportunities exist for formal and informal interaction between leadership and staff, including staff working 2nd and 3rd shift.				
Opportunities exist for leadership to interact directly with patients and families.				
Managers are held accountable for "walking the walk" of patient-centered care.				
Physicians are held accountable for "walking the walk" of patient-centered care.				
Board members are provided opportunities to interact directly with patients and families.				
Total score out of a possible 26		**Percent of total:**	**%**	

table continues next page

Table G.2 **Snapshot of Implementation of Patient-Centered Care** *(continued)*

	Fully implemented throughout the organization	Partially implemented (in progress or in place in some areas, but not all)	No activity	Not applicable
Communicating effectively with patients and families				
Patients are made aware of how to raise a concern related to patient safety and/or their care while they are hospitalized.				
Patients and families are encouraged to ask questions, and systems are in place to capture questions that arise when caregivers are not present to answer them.				
Systems are in place to assist patients and families in knowing who is providing their care, and what the role is of each person on the care team.				
Total score out of a possible 6		Percent of total:		%
Personalization of care				
Patients are able to make requests for when meals will be served to accommodate their personal schedules and routines.				
Patients are able to make requests for when certain procedures will be performed to accommodate their personal schedules and routines.				
Resources are available to staff to educate them on different cultural beliefs/ traditions related to health and healing.				
Food options are available to meet the preferences of different ethnic groups.				
Food is available for patients and families 24 hours a day.				
Total score out of a possible 10		Percent of total:		%
Continuity of care				
Patients and families are able to participate in rounds.				
Patients and families are able to participate in change-of-shift report.				
Plans of care are written in language that patients and families can understand.				
Opportunities exist for patients and families to meet with multiple members of their health care team, including the nurse and physician.				
Tools are provided to patients to help them manage their medication, medical appointments, and other health care needs.				

table continues next page

The Nurse Workforce in the Eastern Caribbean • http://dx.doi.org/10.1596/978-1-4648-0830-2

Table G.2 Snapshot of Implementation of Patient-Centered Care *(continued)*

	Fully implemented throughout the organization	*Partially implemented (in progress or in place in some areas, but not all)*	*No activity*	*Not applicable*
Patients and families are encouraged to participate in discharge planning from the beginning of hospitalization.				
Processes are in place to reinforce and assess comprehension of information and instructions provided at discharge.				
Total score out of a possible 14		Percent of total:		%
Access to information				
A process is in place whereby patients and family may request additional information on their diagnosis and treatment options.				
Patients have access to their medical records while they are being treated, and are assisted in understanding the information contained in their records.				
Patients are made aware of the opportunity to review their medical records with the support of a health care professional.				
Patients are able to contribute their own progress notes in their medical record.				
Patient education materials appropriate for readers of varying literacy levels and for speakers of different native languages are readily available.				
Patients and families have access to a consumer health library.				
A process is in place to disclose unanticipated outcomes to patients (and family as appropriate).				
Total score out of a possible 14		Percent of total:		%
Family involvement				
"Family" is defined by the patient.				
Visitation is flexible, 24-hour, and patient directed (exceptions may include behavioral health).				
Formalized training/education is available for a patient's loved one who may be providing routine care following discharge.				
A process is in place by which a family member or patient may initiate a rapid response team.				

table continues next page

Table G.2 **Snapshot of Implementation of Patient-Centered Care** *(continued)*

	Fully implemented throughout the organization	Partially implemented (in progress or in place in some areas, but not all)	No activity	Not applicable
Family members are able to remain with the patient during codes and resuscitation.				
Support is provided to patients and families involved in an adverse event.				
Comfortable spaces, equipped with a variety of positive diversions, are available throughout the facility for family use.				
Overnight accommodation is available to loved ones wishing to stay overnight with a patient.				
Support is provided to patients' informal caregivers.				
Total score out of a possible of 18			**Percent of total:**	%
The following spaces create a first impression of welcome, comfort, and healing:				
• Main lobby				
• Emergency department entrance				
• Parking lots/garage				
• Information desk				
• Unit-based nurses' stations				
Patients are given privacy during check-in, changing, and treatment.				
For hospitals with semiprivate rooms, space is available for patients to have a private conversation.				
Patients are able to adjust the lighting and temperature in their rooms on their own.				
Patient rooms have views to the outdoors.				
Lounge areas are available in which patients and visitors may congregate.				
A range of diversionary activities, beyond the television, is available to patients and families.				
Overhead paging has been eliminated (with the exception of emergent needs).				
Pleasant-smelling, nontoxic cleaning products are used.				
Signage reflects primary languages of populations served, and uses icons to aid comprehension.				
Patients can easily find their way from the parking areas to their destination.				
Total score out of a possible of 30			**Percent of total:**	%

table continues next page

Table G.2 Snapshot of Implementation of Patient-Centered Care *(continued)*

	Fully implemented throughout the organization	*Partially implemented (in progress or in place in some areas, but not all)*	*No activity*	*Not applicable*
Spiritual needs				
Resources are available to staff to educate them on religious beliefs/traditions related to health and healing.				
Spiritual assessments look beyond a patient's faith traditions to also capture what comforts and centers them.				
Space is available for both quiet contemplation and communal worship.				
Total score out of a possible of 6			**Percent of total:**	**%**
Integrative medicine				
Complementary and integrative therapies are available based on patient interest and community utilization patterns.				
Total score out of a possible of 2			**Percent of total:**	**%**
Community needs				
Space is made available within the facility for community groups to meet.				
Free health-related lectures, wellness clinics, health fairs, and so on are routinely offered to the public.				
Total score out of a possible of 4			**Percent of total:**	**%**
Caregiver needs				
Staff's stress-reduction and wellness needs are addressed.				
Staff is routinely acknowledged for their good work by leadership, peers, and patients and families.				
Staff have opportunities to provide input into ways to enhance the work environment.				
Space is available for staff to decompress between handling patients.				
Support is provided to staff involved in an adverse event.				
Healthy food is available to all staff, including those who work on weekends and nights.				
Total score out of a possible of 12			**Percent of total:**	**%**

Patient Experience Questionnaires

Patient experience questionnaire 2000 (Steine, Finset, and Laerum 2001). Tables G.3, G.4, and G.5 focus on the beneficiary by providing a snapshot of the patient experience directly.

Patient Experience Questionnaire 1

To provide better service, we ask about your experience during this medical visit, what it felt like for you, and what you think it will mean to you and your health situation. Answer all questions, even if you saw your doctor without any specific ailment or problem in mind.

Table G.3 Patient Knowledge Following Visit

Outcome of this specific visit	Please put a (✓) tick in the box that applies	
Do you now know what to do to reduce your health problems or how to prevent further health problems?	Much more	
	Some more	
	A bit more	
	Not much more	
	No more	
Do you know what to expect from now on?	Much more	
	Some more	
	A bit more	
	Not much more	
	No more	
Will you able to handle your health problems differently?	Much more	
	Some more	
	A bit more	
	Not much more	
	No more	
Will it lead to fewer health problems or help you to prevent such problems?	Much more	
	Some more	
	A bit more	
	Not much more	
	No more	
Communication experiences		
We had a good talk.	Agree completely	
	Agree	
	Neutral	
	Disagree	
	Disagree completely	
I felt reassured.	Agree completely	
	Agree	
	Neutral	
	Disagree	
	Disagree completely	

table continues next page

Table G.3 Patient Knowledge Following Visit *(continued)*

Outcome of this specific visit	*Please put a (✓) tick in the box that applies*	
The doctor understood what was on my mind.	Agree completely	
	Agree	
	Neutral	
	Disagree	
	Disagree completely	
I felt I was taken of	Agree completely	
	Agree	
	Neutral	
	Disagree	
	Disagree completely	
It was difficult to connect with the doctor.	Agree completely	
	Agree	
	Neutral	
	Disagree	
	Disagree completely	
Too much time was spent on small talk.	Agree completely	
	Agree	
	Neutral	
	Disagree	
	Disagree completely	
It was difficult to ask questions.	Agree completely	
	Agree	
	Neutral	
	Disagree	
	Disagree completely	
Important decisions were made over my head.	Agree completely	
	Agree	
	Neutral	
	Disagree	
	Disagree completely	
Experience with auxiliary staff		
I sensed that other patients could listen in when I was talking to the staff.	Agree completely	
	Agree	
	Neutral	
	Disagree	
	Disagree completely	
I felt like one of the crowd.	Agree completely	
	Agree	
	Neutral	
	Disagree	
	Disagree completely	

table continues next page

Table G.3 Patient Knowledge Following Visit *(continued)*

Reaction after visit (circle one number in each line)

Relieved	1	2	3	4	5	6	7	Worried
Sad	1	2	3	4	5	6	7	Cheerful
Strengthened	1	2	3	4	5	6	7	Worn out
Relaxed	1	2	3	4	5	6	7	Tense

Patient Experience Questionnaire 2
Table G.4 Form 1: Patient Perception on Patient Centeredness

Please circle the response that best represents your opinion.

To what extent was your main problem(s) discussed today?
Completely   Mostly   A little   Not at all

Would you say that your doctor knows that this was one of your reasons for coming in today?
Yes   Probably   Unsure   No

To what extent did the doctor understand the importance of your reason for coming in today?
Completely   Mostly   A little   Not at all

How well do you think your doctor understood you today?
Very well   Well   Somewhat   Not at all

How satisfied were you with the discussion of your problem?
Very satisfied   Satisfied   Somewhat satisfied   Not satisfied

To what extent did the doctor explain this problem to you?
Completely   Mostly   A little   Not at all

To what extent did you agree with the doctor's opinion about the problem?
Completely   Mostly   A little   Not at all

How much opportunity did you have to ask your questions?
A lot   A fair amount   A little   Not at all

To what extent did the doctor ask about your goals for treatment?
Completely   Mostly   A little   Not at all

To what extent did the doctor explain treatment?
Very well   Well   Somewhat   Not at all

To what extent did the doctor explore how manageable this treatment would be for you?
Completely   Mostly   A little   Not at all

To what extent did you and the doctor discuss your respective roles?
Completely   Mostly   A little   Not at all

To what extent did the doctor encourage you to take the role you wanted in your own care?
Completely   Mostly   A little   Not at all

How much would you say that this doctor cares about you as a person?
Very much   A fair amount   A little   Not at all

Source: Centre for Studies in Family Medicine.

The Nurse Workforce in the Eastern Caribbean • http://dx.doi.org/10.1596/978-1-4648-0830-2

Patient Experience Questionnaire 3
Table G.5 Form 2: Patient Feedback on Communication with Physicians

Please circle the response that best represents your opinion.

To what extent was your main problem(s) discussed today?

| Completely | Mostly | A little | Not at all |

How satisfied were you with the discussion of your problem?

| Very satisfied | Satisfied | Somewhat satisfied | Not satisfied |

To what extent did the doctor listen to what you had to say?

| Completely | Mostly | A little | Not at all |

To what extent did the doctor explain this problem to you?

| Completely | Mostly | A little | Not at all |

To what extent did you and the doctor discuss your respective roles?

| Completely | Mostly | A little | Not at all |

To what extent did the doctor explain treatment?

| Very well | Well | Somewhat | Not at all |

To what extent did the doctor explore how manageable this treatment would be for you?

| Completely | Mostly | A little | Not at all |

How well do you think your doctor understood you today?

| Very well | Well | Somewhat | Not at all |

To what extent did the doctor discuss personal or family issues that might affect your health?

| Completely | Mostly | A little | Not at all |

Source: Centre for Studies in Family Medicine.

Physician Perception Questionnaire
Table G.6 Form 3: Physician Assessment

Please circle the response that best represents your opinion.

To what extent was your patient's main problem(s) discussed today?

| Completely | Mostly | A little | Not at all |

How satisfied were you with the discussion of your patient's problem?

| Very satisfied | Satisfied | Somewhat satisfied | Not satisfied |

To what extent did you listen to what your patient had to say?

| Completely | Mostly | A little | Not at all |

To what extent did you explain the problem to the patient?

| Completely | Mostly | A little | Not at all |

To what extent did you and the patient discuss your respective roles?

| Completely | Mostly | A little | Not at all |

To what extent did you explain treatment?

| Very well | Well | Somewhat | Not at all |

To what extent did you and the patient explore how manageable this treatment would be for the patient?

| Completely | Mostly | A little | Not at all |

table continues next page

Table G.6 **Form 3: Physician Assessment** *(continued)*

How well do you think you understood the patient today?			
Very well	Well	Somewhat	Not at all

Regarding today's problem, to what extent did you discuss personal or family issues that might be affecting your patient's health?			
Completely	Mostly	A little	Not at all

Source: Centre for Studies in Family Medicine.

References

Epstein, R. M., and E. M. Hundert. 2002. "Defining and Assessing Professional Competence." *Journal of the American Medical Association* 287 (2): 226–35.

Frampton, S., S. Guastello, C. Brady, M. Hale, S. Horowitz, and others 2008. *Patient-Centered Care Improvement Guide*. Boston, MA: Picker Institute.

Steine, S., A. Finset, and E. Laerum. 2001. "A New, Brief Questionnaire (PEQ) Developed in Primary Health Care for Measuring Patients' Experience of Interaction, Emotion and Consultation Outcome." *Family Practice* 18 (4): 410–18.

IOM (Institute of Medicine). 2003. *Health Professions Education: A Bridge to Quality*. Washington, DC : National Academies Press.

WHO (World Health Organization). 2002. *Innovative Care for Chronic Conditions. Building Blocks for Action*. Geneva: WHO.

Toolkit for Using Informatics

Background

Health care informatics is more than information technology: It is the development and application of information technology systems to problems in health care, research, and education. Through the use of such tools, the Institute of Medicine suggests that health professionals will be able to perform four key tasks (IOM 2003): reduce errors, manage knowledge and information, make decisions, and communicate more effectively.

Definitions

Human resources for health. The World Health Organization's definition includes all people engaged in actions whose primary intent is to enhance health. These include public and private sector nurses, doctors, midwives, and pharmacists, as well as technicians and other paraprofessionals.

Competencies. These are the habitual and judicious use of communication, knowledge, technical skills, clinical reasoning, emotions, values, and reflection in daily practice (Epstein and Hundert 2002).

Four Key Tasks

This section examines the four key tasks of reducing errors, managing knowledge and information, making decisions, and communicating more effectively.

Reducing Errors

Computerized medical records and prescription systems eliminate handwritten information, which is critical to error reduction. E-mail communication, electronic medical records, and computer-aided decision-support systems also offer the potential to improve care across clinicians and settings, thus reducing the chances of errors from poor coordination.

Managing Knowledge and Information

Online databases make it possible for health professionals to access the knowledge base and literature sources needed to conduct evidence-based practice. Open-source software enables the development of on-site databases or disease registries, which can assist with the development of population-based public health solutions.

Making Decisions

Computerized decision-support systems are reminders to help primary health care teams comply with evidence-based practice guidelines, and are sources of feedback to providers to show how they are performing on care measures. Such systems have been effective in encouraging physician compliance with recommended guidelines that support improved drug prescribing, dosing, treatment, prevention, administration, and monitoring.

Communication

In time, e-mail, and mobile phone technologies will be used to send appointment reminder messages, discuss prescription renewals, notify patients of test results, and provide advice and reassurance. The Internet also allows for the creation of

Table H.1 Informatics Competencies Required of Human Resources for Health

Competency	Does competency need development? (yes/no)
The following general informatics competencies are relevant to all human resources for health:	
Using word-processing and data analysis software	
Searching online and internal databases	
Retrieving and managing data	
Being aware of data security systems related to the use of patient information	
Designing and using patient registries	
Communication	
Use of e-mail for communication with colleagues	
Use of e-mail for communication with patients	
Use of mobile phones for communication with colleagues	
Use of mobile phones for communication with patients	
Is there a national website for health information?	
Existing information and communication technology environment	*Yes/no*
Are electronic medical records used?	
Are electronic personnel records used?	
Are electronic staff-training records used?	
What percentage of staff have access to a computer?	
What percentage of staff have access to the internet?	
What percentage of staff can communicate routinely with colleagues?	
Is the Internet speed adequate enough to support conference calls via voice over IP (for example, Skype)?	

special interest groups of patients and human resources for health, which can be used to facilitate the self-management needed for better disease control.

However, certain legal and regulatory issues need to be addressed before the widespread use of informatics can become a reality. Thus health professionals need to know and understand how to protect access to provider-patient communications. Evolving issues related to the use of informatics by health care professionals include the need for data standards so that data can be shared across settings, decisions about who should have access to patient-based information, documentation of provider-patient communications in patient records, and medical practice liability concerns (NCVHS 2000) (table H.1).

References

Epstein, R. M., and E. M. Hundert. 2002. "Defining and Assessing Professional Competence." *Journal of the American Medical Association* 287 (2): 226–35.

IOM (Institute of Medicine). 2003. *Health Professions Education: A Bridge to Quality.* Washington, DC: National Academies Press.

NCVHS (National Committee on Vital and Health Statistics). 2000. *Uniform Data Standards for Patient Medical Record Information.* Hyattsville, MD: NCVHS.

Toolkit for Supporting Quality Improvement

Background

Health services are facing significant challenges. As populations increase and life expectancy improves, the demand for health care is outstripping the staffing and financial resources available (WHO 2002). Consequently, health care needs to improve the efficiency and quality of care, enabling limited resources to be used more effectively.

The Institute of Medicine recommends the following core domains for competency that are relevant to all human resources for health (HRH):

- Patient-centered care
- Interdisciplinary teams
- Evidence-based practice
- Quality improvement
- Informatics

Definitions

Human resources for health. The World Health Organization's definition includes all people engaged in actions whose primary intent is to enhance health. These include public and private sector nurses, doctors, midwives, and pharmacists, as well as technicians and other paraprofessionals.

Competencies. These are the habitual and judicious use of communication, knowledge, technical skills, clinical reasoning, emotions, values, and reflection in daily practice (Epstein and Hundert 2002).

Continuous quality improvement. This can be defined briefly as a comprehensive management philosophy that focuses on continuous improvement by applying scientific methods to gain knowledge and control over variation in work processes (Tindill and Stewart 1993, 209–20).

This appendix focuses on prioritizing and assessing the competencies pertaining to quality improvement.

Quality Improvement Competencies

Continuous quality improvement is one a range of techniques that can be used to improve health care. Other techniques include clinical audits, best practice guidelines, evidence-based medicine, targets, national service frameworks, and performance management. But these alone cannot force change. Although continuous quality improvement is a broad concept, it is essential to the improvement of health services, whether in primary, secondary, or tertiary care. This is reflected by quality improvement as a competency being recommended by several health-related professional bodies (WHO 2005). And it is an approach that can be adopted at an individual or organizational level.

The key documents used to create the competency lists shown in table I.1 for quality improvement were Batalden, Berwick, and Bisognano's (1998)

Table I.1 Competencies and Knowledge Domains for Quality Improvement

Institute for Healthcare Improvement	Institute of Medicine	World Health Organization
Customer/beneficiary knowledge: identifying people or groups using health care and assessing their needs and preferences.	Assess current practices and compare them with better practices to identify opportunities for improvement.	Translating evidence into practice
Variation and measurement: using measurement to understand variation in performance to improve the design of health care.	Design and test interventions to change the process of care, with the objective of improving quality.	Measuring care delivery and outcomes
	Identify errors and hazards in care; understand and implement basic safety design principles, such as standardization and simplification and human factors training.	Translating evidence into practice
Leading and making change in health care: methods and skills for making change in complex organizations, including the strategic management of people and their work.	n.a.	Learning and adapting to change
Health care as process/system: acknowledging the interdependence of service users, procedures, activities, and technologies that come together to meet the needs of individuals and communities.	Continually understand and measure quality of care in terms of (1) structure, or the inputs into the system; (2) process, or the interactions between clinicians and patients; and (3) outcomes, or evidence about changes in patients' health status in relation to patient and community needs.	n.a.

table continues next page

Table I.1 **Competencies and Knowledge Domains for Quality Improvement** *(continued)*

Institute for Healthcare Improvement	Institute of Medicine	World Health Organization
Collaboration: knowledge and skills needed to work effectively in groups. Understand the perspectives and responsibilities of others.	Act as an effective member of an interdisciplinary team, and improve the quality of one's own performance through self-assessment and personal change.	n.a.
Developing new, locally useful knowledge: recognizing and being able to develop new knowledge, including through empirical testing.	n.a.	n.a.
Social context and accountability: understanding the social context of health care, including financing.	n.a.	n.a.
Professional subject matter: having relevant professional knowledge and an ability to apply and connect the other seven domains. This includes core competencies published by professional boards and accrediting organizations.	n.a.	n.a.

Sources: Batalden, Berwick, and Bisognano 1998; IOM 2003; WHO 2005.
Note: n.a. = not applicable.

Knowledge Domains for Health Professional Students Seeking Competency in the Continual Improvement and Innovation of Health Care; the Institute of Medicine's *Health Professions Education: A Bridge to Quality* (IOM 2003); and the World Health Organization's *Preparing a Health Care Workforce for the 21st Century: The Challenge of Chronic Conditions* (WHO 2005).

It should be noted that the domains considered by the Institute of Healthcare Improvement are related to knowledge rather than competencies, and WHO's competencies are aimed at improving the care of chronic conditions.

Use the questionnaires to assess departmental quality improvement readiness. The individual Continuous Quality Improvement Questionnaire is for experiences and attitudes toward quality improvement. The results of these surveys will help you to conduct a competency needs assessment, which can then be reviewed in light of the identified priority competencies.

Department Initial Readiness Assessment

Determining a clinic's readiness to implement an intervention is a critical first step to facilitation. This questionnaire in table I.2 was developed based on the Health Resources and Services Administration document on quality improvement,[1] and findings from the Agency for Healthcare Research and Quality's 2010 Practice Facilitation Consensus Meeting.[2] Both are part of the U.S. Department of Health and Human Services. Table I.3 shows the Continuous Quality Improvement Questionnaire.

Table I.2 Checklist for Assessing Practice Readiness

For each question circle the appropriate response

Is there an organizational commitment to quality improvement?	Yes	No	Not sure
Does the organization have a structure to assess and improve quality of care?	Yes	No	Not sure
Do you think the organization is willing and able to identify an "improvement" champion who will be the facilitator's point person?	Yes	No	Not sure
Does the organization have resources dedicated to quality improvement activities?	Yes	No	Not sure
Has the organization identified barriers to fully implement a quality improvement program?	Yes	No	Not sure
Are there effective and functioning communication channels between leadership, staff, and teams?	Yes	No	Not sure
Do you think that the organizational leadership is interested in specific or general improvement, as evidenced by requests for assistance or receptiveness to receiving facilitation to support improvement?	Yes	No	Not sure
Do you think the organizational leadership is willing to participate in ongoing communication with a facilitator and be part of the quality improvement team?	Yes	No	Not sure
Do you think the leadership is willing to provide protected time for key staff to engage in improvement work?	Yes	No	Not sure
Do you think the leadership has sufficient knowledge of quality improvement principles, methodologies, and change management?	Yes	No	Not sure
Do clinical staff work well in multidisciplinary teams?	Yes	No	Not sure
Does the organization routinely and systematically collect and analyze data to assess quality of care?	Yes	No	Not sure
Do providers and staff have a basic understanding of quality improvement tools and techniques?	Yes	No	Not sure
Do providers and staff understand their roles, responsibilities, and expectations for quality improvement activities?	Yes	No	Not sure
Do you think the clinic teams are willing to meet regularly as a quality improvement team, and members follow through with this plan?	Yes	No	Not sure
Do you think the clinic teams are willing to gather and report data on practice performance on key metrics?	Yes	No	Not sure
Do you think the clinic has sufficient organizational and financial stability to avoid becoming too distracted or overwhelmed by competing demands or financial concerns?	Yes	No	Not sure
Do you think the clinic is not engaged in other large-scale improvement projects, and does not have other demanding competing priorities?	Yes	No	Not sure

Table I.3 Individual Continuous Quality Improvement Questionnaire

1	Have you ever attended any workshop related to continuous quality improvement (CQI)?	Yes			
		No		Go to Q3	
2	If yes, please indicate when you last attended a CQI workshop.	Less than 1 year ago			
		1–2 years ago			
		Over 2 years ago			
3	Have you participated in a CQI project in the last 3 years?	Yes			
		No			
4	Do you tend to disagree or agree with the statement: I have a basic understanding of the principles of CQI.	Agree			
		Disagree			
		Undecided			

5. The following statements relate to health care and quality improvement. Please indicate by marking a tick in the box that most closely indicates the extent to which you agree or disagree with these statements.

SA = Strongly agree, A = Agree, N = Neither agree nor disagree, D = Disagree; SD = Strongly disagree

	SA	A	N	D	SD
A successful health care organization maintains a clear focus on those it serves.					
Quality improvement should focus on work processes rather than individual performance.					
It is desirable to build assessment and data collection in health care processes.					
It is important to use multidisciplinary teams as the mechanism for introducing improvement in health care processes.					
Most problems originate because of poor performance by individual staff members.					
In health care, it is not important to reduce variation in clinical practice.					

6. Please indicate the extent to which each of the following factors would be important in your decision to participate in a continuous quality improvement project (CQI).

SA = Strongly agree, A = Agree, N = Neither agree nor disagree, D = Disagree, SD = Strongly disagree

	SA	A	N	D	SD
CQI project endorsed by respected clinical colleague					
CQI project relevant to my area of clinical practice					
Availability of a CQI project coordinator to arrange project activities					
CQI project directly affects any clinical practice					
Incentives for health professionals who participate in CQI projects					
CQI project endorsed by hospital administration					
Time commitment involved in undertaking CQI project					
CQI project that introduces only minimal changes to current clinical practice					

Do you agree or disagree with the following questions? Please put a tick in the appropriate box.

D = disagree, A = agree, U = undecided	D	A	U
7 CQI is of limited value to improving health care			
8 CQI is a positive trend in health care			
9 The primary goal of a hospital CQI project is to reduce health care costs			
10 CQI is motivated by a desire to take patient preference with consideration			
11 CQI projects are a challenge to professional autonomy			

Source: Hill and others 2001.

Notes

1. The original quality improvement document is available at http://www.ahrq.gov /professionals/prevention-chronic-care/improve/system/pfhandbook/mod12 .html#knox2010.

2. See http://www.ahrq.gov/professionals/prevention-chronic-care/improve/system /pfhandbook/mod12.html#knox2010 for more details.

References

Batalden, P., D. Berwick, and M. Bisognano. 1998. *Knowledge Domains for Health Professional Students Seeking Competency in the Continual Improvement and Innovation of Health Care*. Boston, MA: Institute for Healthcare Improvement.

Epstein, R. M., and E. M. Hundert. 2002. "Defining and Assessing Professional Competence." *Journal of the American Medical Association* 287 (2): 226–35.

Hill, A., F. Gwadry-Sridhar, T. Armstrong, and W. J. Sibbald. 2001. "Development of the Continuous Quality Improvement Questionnaire (CQIQ)." *Journal of Critical Care* 16 (4): 150–60.

IOM (Institute of Medicine). 2003. *Health Professions Education: A Bridge to Quality*. Washington, DC: National Academies Press.

Tindill, B. S., and D. W. Stewart. 1993. "Integration of Total Quality and Quality Assurance." In *The Textbook of Total Quality in Healthcare*, edited by A. F. Al-Assaf and J. A. Schmele. Delray Beach, FL: St. Lucie Press.

WHO (World Health Organization). 2002. *Innovative Care for Chronic Conditions: Building Blocks for Action*. Geneva: WHO.

———. 2005. *Preparing a Health Care Workforce for the 21st Century: The Challenge of Chronic Conditions*. Geneva: WHO.

Human Resources for Health Governance in the Eastern Caribbean

Introduction

Human resources for health (HRH) in the Eastern Caribbean are governed by global, regional, and country-level policies, initiatives, and legislation that are supported by instruments focusing on labor legislation, international recruitment, and noncommunicable diseases (NCDs). This appendix is an inventory of the policies, initiatives, legislation, and instruments governing HRH in the Eastern Caribbean that may affect how the health workforce can be strengthened to address NCDs.

Global HRH Initiatives

The World Health Organization's *World Health Report 2006: Working Together for Health* (WHO 2006) issued recommendations for countries to build high-performing workforces for national health systems to respond to current and emerging challenges. The report also detailed the need to develop national strategic plans and engage in strategic HRH planning.

Since 2008, three global forums have been held to address HRH needs worldwide, bringing together more than 1,000 health care policy makers, experts, and advocates. In 2008, the Kampala Declaration was announced at the First Global Forum on Human Resources for Health in Uganda. This called on governments, in cooperation with international organizations, academic institutions, civil society, the private sector, professional associations, and other partners, to "create health workforce information systems, to improve research and to develop capacity for data management in order to institutionalize evidence-based decision-making and enhance shared learning" (WHO and Global Health Workforce Alliance 2008, 11).

The Second Global Forum on Human Resources for Health, held in Bangkok in 2011, reviewed the progress since the Kampala Declaration and made a renewed commitment to strengthen the global health workforce. The decision coming out of the forum was that "people, everywhere, shall have access to a skilled, motivated and supported health worker within a robust health system" (WHO and Global Health Workforce Alliance 2011). The following practical needs were identified at the forum:

- In countries with HRH shortages, the full range of public policies that influence the supply of and demand for the health workforce, enhance preservice training through the adoption of emerging best practices, and ensure the poor and marginalized get equitable access to quality services, should be used.
- Increased education and training capacity to match the growing demand for HRH.
- Reliable and updated information, particularly for retention, gender balance, minimum standards, and competency frameworks.

The third Global Forum on Human Resources for Health, held in 2003 in Recife, had "Human Resources for Health: Foundation for Universal Health Coverage and the Post-2015 Development Agenda" as its theme. Outcomes are pending.

Regional HRH Initiatives

Much work has been done on describing the baseline situation for regional HRH in the Caribbean, an effort driven jointly by technical cooperation involving Caribbean member states and regional donor organizations. This section looks at some regional HRH initiates over the past three decades.

Caribbean Cooperation in Health

Initiated in 1984, the Caribbean Cooperation in Health (CCH) was designed to improve regional health through collaboration and technical cooperation, and is in its third phase. Under the first phase starting in 1984, the CCH aimed to close gaps in the regional health agenda. The second phase, starting in 1992, set goals and targets for improving seven areas: communicable and noncommunicable diseases, health systems, environmental health, food and nutrition, mental health, family and child health, and human resources development. The ongoing third phase continues work in these areas and supports country efforts toward regional public goods and services, and national strategic directions. The revitalization of primary health care provides the framework for guiding health developments. The mandate of the third phase is orientated toward the following:

- People-centered development
- Genuine stakeholder and community participation and involvement
- Effective regional coordination and public health leadership

- Outcome-oriented planning and implementation, and performance-based monitoring
- Resource mobilization for health, health coverage, and social protection for the people of the region

In addition, the CCH's third phase has the guiding principles of the right to the highest attainable level of health, equity, solidarity, people-centered care, and leadership. Of these, the last two have direct relevance to strengthening HRH and achieving the fourth goal of the third phase (adequate human resource capacity to support health development in the region). The third phase recognizes that people-centered care is key to developing healthy communities. The guiding principle of leadership identifies public health leadership as a priority and vital to improving performance and the attainment of "health for all."

Toronto Call to Action

In 2005, the Toronto Call to Action for a Decade of Human Resources in Health in the Americas was launched (PAHO and Health Canada 2005). Sponsored by the Pan American Health Organization (PAHO), WHO, and Health Canada, this initiative aims to mobilize institutional actors, both national and international, in all relevant sectors and civil society to collectively strengthen HRH through policies and interventions in accordance with national health priorities to provide access to quality health services for all the peoples of the Americas by 2015. Although the challenges are multiple, they can be grouped into five main areas, which require the following actions:

- *Long range planning.* Define long-range policies and plans to better adapt the health workforce so that it will be prepared to meet expected changes in the health systems, and to improve the institutional capacity for defining these policies and revising them periodically.
- *Getting the right people in the right places.* Deploy the appropriate personnel in the right positions and in the right areas to achieve an equitable distribution of the quantity and skill sets of health workers in different regions so that they match the specific health needs of the populations they are serving.
- *Regulating migration.* Regulate the migration and displacement of health workers to ensure access to health care for the entire population.
- *Labor relations.* Generate labor relationships between health workers and organizations promoting healthy work environments, and foster commitment to the institutional mission to guarantee quality health services for the entire population.
- *Cooperation between health training and health services.* Develop mechanisms of cooperation between training institutions (universities and schools) and health services institutions so that it is possible to adapt the education of health workers to a universal and equitable model of providing quality care to meet the health needs of the entire population.

The Toronto call to action was the catalyst for the development of PAHO's core dataset for HRH monitoring, and the follow-up development of the indicators for the 20 HRH goals. The baseline for these goals was measured from 2008 to 2011, culminating in an important summary report for the Eastern Caribbean, which was used as a source document for the HRH profiles of the four case country studies in this report.

Needham's Point Declaration

In 2007, Caribbean Community's (CARICOM) heads of government issued a declaration at Needham's Point, Barbados, stating that functional cooperation is one of the principal means by which the benefits of integration will be distributed throughout the community (CARICOM 2007a). The heads of government pledged to invest in functional cooperation for the further development of the region's human and social capital.

Health Agenda for the Americas

In 2008, ministers of health launched the Health Agenda for the Americas 2008–15 at the 47th Directing Council of PAHO (resolution CD47.R3). The agenda expressed the shared vision to strengthen the management and development of HRH as a way to improve health. To define this vision, health ministers, in 2007, adopted 20 regional goals at the 27th Pan American Sanitary Conference (resolution CSP27/10). These were based on the core values and elements of a health system based on primary health care. Building on the work of this resolution, the directing council reviewed and adopted the policy document "Increasing Access to Qualified Health Workers in Primary Health Care-Based Health Systems" in 2013. This identifies the policy reforms and reorientation needed to improve access to trained and skilled primary health care workers, and highlights the need for developing new models of HRH governance and strengthening HRH planning capacity.

PAHO Core Reports and WHO/PAHO 20G Reports

From 2009 to 2012, PAHO published a series of so-called *core reports* quantifying the numbers of health professionals in Caribbean countries (reported per 10,000 population); these reports relate to the PAHO/WHO 20 goals for monitoring HRH and are known as the *20G reports*. Most contributing countries had both a core report and a 20G report,[1] as well as a summary comparison report prepared in 2012 reviewing regional progress toward the PAHO/WHO 20 goals.

USAID Health Systems 20/20 Reports

From 2006 to 2012, the U.S. Agency for International Development (USAID) funded the Health Systems 20/20 cooperative agreement, which helped USAID-supported countries overcome barriers to using life-saving priority health services. Health Systems 20/20 worked to strengthen health systems through integrated approaches for improving financing, governance, and operations, and for building the sustainable capacity of institutions. As part of this initiative, country situational analyses were published on Antigua and Barbuda, Dominica, Grenada, Guyana, St. Lucia, and St. Vincent and the Grenadines. Together, the PAHO and USAID initiatives provide a comprehensive HRH situational analysis for some Caribbean countries. PAHO's reports focus on the quantitative assessment of HRH staffing levels, and USAID's reports on legislative and policy infrastructure as it relates to HRH.

The situational analysis and roadmap development is being done for the countries that benefited from both PAHO and USAID baseline reports, and whose reports have been ratified at the national level and made publicly available by the donor organization. Table J.1 shows the availability of the baseline reports in Caribbean countries. The four countries with reports from both PAHO and USAID—this publication's case study countries—are used to provide an assessment of the NCD burden, an HRH situational assessment, and an HRH roadmap for change. Ultimately, however, this process must be completed for all countries wanting to enact HRH change.

Table J.1 Availability of PAHO and USAID HRH Country-Level Baseline Reports

Country	PAHO core data	PAHO 20 goals	USAID
Anguilla	Completed and publicly available	Completed and publicly available	No report
Antigua and Barbuda	Completed but not publicly available	Completed but not publicly available	Completed and publicly available
Barbados	Completed and publicly available	Completed and publicly available	No report
Belize	Completed and publicly available	Completed and publicly available	No report
Dominica	Completed and publicly available	Completed and publicly available	Completed and publicly available
Grenada	Completed and publicly available	Completed but not publicly available	Completed and publicly available
Guyana	No report	No report	Completed and publicly available
Jamaica	Completed and publicly available	Completed and publicly available	No report
Montserrat	Completed and publicly available	Completed and publicly available	No report
St. Kitts and Nevis	Completed but not publicly available	Completed but not publicly available	Completed and publicly available
St. Lucia	Completed and publicly available	Completed but not publicly available	Completed and publicly available
St. Vincent and the Grenadines	Completed and publicly available	No report	Completed and publicly available
Trinidad and Tobago	Completed but not publicly available	Completed and publicly available	No report

Source: PAHO, USAID country-level baseline reports.
Note: HRH = human resources for health; PAHO = Pan American Health Organization; USAID = U.S. Agency for International Development.

International Legal Agreements and Obligations Governing Policies for Health

Two basic types of international legal instruments covering health are used: legally binding instruments or treaties, and non-legally binding instruments. The former create obligations and corresponding duties of compliance between parties or signatory states under international law; the latter represent a political commitment or agreement between states that is not legally enforceable, but may still create expectations of compliance.

Legally Binding Instruments Governing Policies for HRH

Three multilateral treaties govern policies affecting HRH in English-speaking CARICOM countries (Kurowski and others 2012):

- *General Agreement on Trade in Services.* This is a multilateral treaty that governs all World Trade Organization members. It prohibits discrimination in the hiring of HRH on the basis of nationality; however, a World Trade Organization member can show a preference for hiring health personnel from a country with which it has a regional trade agreement. The agreement also requires removing restrictions on the free movement of labor.
- *International Labour Organization Migration Conventions.* This provides the means for ensuring the ethical recruitment of health workers. Convention 97 requires that member states accord migrants and nationals the same treatment, irrespective of race, religion, gender, or nationality.
- *CARICOM Single Market and Economy.* This multifaceted plan to integrate CARICOM economies aims to remove obstacles to the free movement of labor and services, and can influence HRH policy. The Revised Treaty of Chaguaramas, which established CARICOM, calls for the development of common standards for accreditation and equivalency of qualifications, and for harmonizing social services such as education and health.

Country-level obligations under these legally binding international agreements (table J.2) do not limit a range of approaches to managing migration. However, they do not address country or regional policy priority areas concerning HRH or NCD prevention and management.

Non-Legally Binding Instruments Governing Policies for HRH

Three non-legally binding instruments govern policies that affect HRH in CARICOM's English-speaking countries (Kurowski and others 2012):

- *Regional Plan for Action for Human Resources for Health 2007–15.*[2] Comprehensive and broad in scope, this declaration requests that member states develop a sophisticated national plan, with specialized competencies within ministries of health to deal with health personnel policies at the national and local levels. In particular, it focuses on meeting specific strategic goals as

Table J.2 Obligations under Legally Binding International Agreements Affecting HRH

Agreement	Signatories	Obligations	Comments
General Agreement on Trade in Services	Antigua and Barbuda, The Bahamas, Barbados, Belize, Dominica, Grenada, Guyana, Jamaica, St. Kitts and Nevis, St. Lucia, St. Vincent and the Grenadines, Trinidad and Tobago	Not to discriminate in hiring HRH on the basis of nationality without preexisting regional trade agreement. Remove restrictions on free movement of labor	Exempts services provided on a noncommercial and competitive basis
International Labour Organization Convention 97	The Bahamas, Barbados, Belize, Dominica, Grenada, Guyana, Jamaica, St. Lucia, Trinidad and Tobago	Provide migrants with treatment no less favorable than given to nationals	n.a.
Caribbean Single Market Economy	Antigua and Barbuda, The Bahamas, Barbados, Belize, Dominica, Grenada, Guyana, Jamaica, St. Kitts and Nevis, St. Lucia, St. Vincent and the Grenadines, Trinidad and Tobago	Free movement of services and labor. Mutual recognition of diplomas, certificates, and other evidence of qualifications	Provides for exemptions when the rights granted would create serious economic hardship

Source: Kurowski and others 2012.
Note: HRH = human resources for health; n.a. = not applicable.

part of a 10-year human resources plan adapted to each country's situation. It also requests that the director of PAHO promote and facilitate technical and financial cooperation between the countries, and support the plans of action.

- *Commonwealth Code of Practice for the International Recruitment of Health Workers.* This was launched in 2003 in response to HRH shortages, particularly in small island states, and remote and rural areas. The code aims to provide a framework for international recruitment with special consideration of the effects of international HRH recruitment on developing countries. It recommends that countries experiencing shortages of health worker should not be targeted by other countries for HRH recruitment, and it encourages ethical recruitment that safeguards the rights of recruits.

- *WHO Global Code of Practice on the International Recruitment of Health Personnel.* Launched in 2010, this was designed by WHO member states to serve as a continuous and dynamic framework for global dialogue and cooperation on the international recruitment of HRH. The code establishes and promotes voluntary principles and practices for the ethical international recruitment of HRH. Member states are discouraged from actively recruiting staff from developing countries facing critical shortages of health workers. The code also aims to facilitate the strengthening of health systems.

NCD Instruments and Initiatives

This section looks at the international and regional efforts to develop policies for tackling the increasing burden of NCDs in the Caribbean.

Nassau Declaration and Caribbean Commission on Health and Development Report

In 2001, the Nassau Declaration of CARICOM Heads of Government—"The Health of the Region is the Wealth of the Region"—gave rise to the Caribbean Commission on Health and Development in 2003. Its 2005 report showed the major health problems of the region were chronic diseases, HIV/AIDS, and injuries and violence. The commission also highlighted three critical issues: public health leadership, workforce capacity, and health information systems.

Joint PAHO and WHO Strategy on Chronic Diseases

In 2006, PAHO and WHO came out with the Regional Strategy on an Integrated Approach to the Prevention and Control of Chronic Diseases Including Diet, Physical Activity, and Health, which was approved by Caribbean countries.

Port of Spain Declaration

Following CARICOM's review of the Caribbean Commission on Health and Development's 2005 report, the CARICOM Summit on Noncommunicable Diseases was convened in 2007, resulting in the Port of Spain Declaration on "Uniting to Stop the Epidemic of Chronic Noncommunicable Diseases." The 15-point declaration outlined a framework for policies and programs across several ministries, in collaboration with the private sector, civil society, the media, nongovernment organizations, academe, and the community for creating supportive environments "to make the right choice the easy choice" (CARICOM 2007b).

Collaborative Action for Risk Factor Reduction and Effective Management of NCDs

In 2007, Caribbean countries requested their minsters of health to apply for membership of the Collaborative Action for Risk Factor Prevention and Effective Management of NCDs (CARMEN) network. The CARMEN network seeks to do the following:

- Implement projects to support the Regional Strategy on an Integrated Approach to the Prevention and Control of Chronic Diseases Including Diet, Physical Activity, and Health
- Define tools and methodologies to support CARMEN initiatives at the country level
- Deepen the sense of joint collaborative commitment among PAHO, countries, and development partners toward implementing the regional strategy

Healthy Caribbean Coalition

In 2008, a regional civil society umbrella organization, the Healthy Caribbean Coalition, was created; it released the Bridgetown Declaration in support of the CARICOM Summit on Noncommunicable Diseases. From the discussions at the 2009 CARMEN meeting, the following priorities were outlined for the Caribbean:

- Support for the design and development of national commissions
- Support for developing tobacco legislation for implementation in CARICOM countries

- Development of an integrated approach to NCDs, and mainstreaming surveillance and other actions within the health care model
- Capacity development for resource mobilization, with the emphasis on grants

Fifth Summit of the Americas

The Fifth Summit of the Americas, held in Port of Spain in Trinidad and Tobago in April 2009, reaffirmed the PAHO/WHO and CARICOM plans, and restated the need for universal access to quality comprehensive health care. The summit declaration reaffirmed the PAHO/WHO and CARICOM plans.

Later in the same year, the problem of NCDs was presented to the Commonwealth Heads of Government Meeting in Port of Spain. Their declaration strongly emphasized the importance of NCD management and committed Commonwealth countries to elevate the priority of NCDs. The heads of government also supported the call for a United Nations High Level Meeting in September 2011.

United Nations High Level Meeting

The meeting's declaration promoted a range of activities, including the reduction of NCD risk factors, the creation of health-promoting environments, and the strengthening of national policies and health systems.

WHO Targets for NCDs

In 2008, WHO published the *2008–13 Action Plan for the Global Strategy for the Prevention and Control of Noncommunicable Diseases* (WHO 2008) (table J.3). This was underpinned by six objectives, which were updated as part of the Global Action Plan for the Prevention and Control of Noncommunicable

Table J.3 WHO Action Plan to Prevent and Control Noncommunicable Diseases, Objectives for 2008 and 2013

2008 Objectives	2013 Objectives
To raise the priority accorded to noncommunicable diseases (NCD) in development work at global and national levels, and to integrate prevention and control of such diseases into policies across all government departments.	To raise the priority accorded to the prevention and control of NCDs in global, regional, and national agendas; and internationally agreed development goals, through strengthened international cooperation and advocacy.
To establish and strengthen national policies and plans for the prevention and control of NCDs.	To strengthen national capacity, leadership, governance, multisectoral action, and partnerships to accelerate country responses for the prevention and control of NCDs.
To promote interventions to reduce the main shared modifiable risk factors for NCDs: tobacco use, unhealthy diets, physical inactivity, and harmful use of alcohol.	To reduce modifiable risk factors for NCDs and underlying social determinants through the creation of health-promoting environments.
To promote research for the prevention and control of NCDs.	To promote and support national capacity for high-quality research and development for the prevention and control of NCDs.

table continues next page

Table J.3 WHO Action Plan to Prevent and Control Noncommunicable Diseases, Objectives for 2008 and 2013 *(continued)*

2008 Objectives	2013 Objectives
To promote partnerships for the prevention and control of NCDs.	To strengthen and orient health systems to address the prevention and control of NCDs and the underlying social determinants through people-centered primary health care and universal health coverage.
To monitor NCDs and their determinants and evaluate progress at the national, regional and global levels.	To monitor the trends and determinants of NCDs and evaluate progress in their prevention and control.

Source: WHO 2008.
Note: NCDs = noncommunicable diseases.

Figure J.1 Timeline for the Development of Caribbean NCD Initiatives

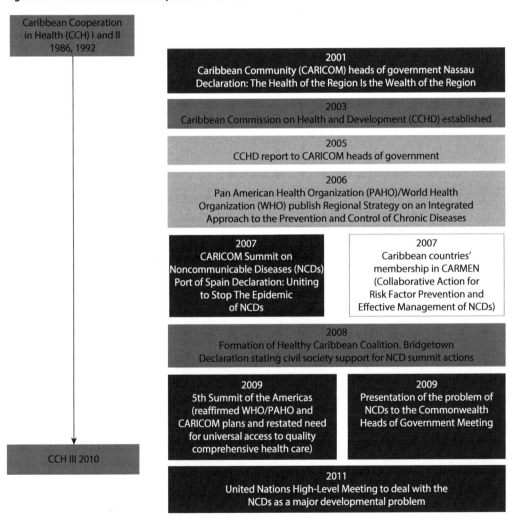

■ High-level meeting ■ Organization established ■ Report published

Diseases 2013–20, endorsed by the 2013 World Health Assembly. These updated objectives are associated with the following voluntary targets:

- 25 percent relative reduction in the risk of premature mortality from cardio-vascular diseases, cancer, diabetes, or chronic respiratory diseases
- 10 percent relative reduction in the harmful use of alcohol, as appropriate, within the national context
- 10 percent relative reduction in the prevalence of insufficient physical activity
- 30 percent relative reduction in mean population intake of salt/sodium
- 30 percent relative reduction in the prevalence of tobacco use in people ages 15 plus
- 25 percent relative reduction in the prevalence of raised blood pressure or contain the prevalence of raised blood pressure, according to national circumstances
- Halt the rise in diabetes and obesity
- At least 50 percent of eligible people receive drug therapy and counseling (including glycemic control) to prevent heart attacks and strokes
- 80 percent availability of the affordable basic technologies and essential medicines, including generics, required to treat major NCDs in public and private facilities

Notes

1. PAHO HRH baseline reports have been prepared for Anguilla, Antigua and Barbuda, Barbados, Belize, Dominica, Grenada, Jamaica, Montserrat, St. Kitts and Nevis, St. Lucia, St. Vincent and the Grenadines, and Trinidad and Tobago.
2. Resolution CE140.R13 adopted during the 140th Session of the Executive Committee of PAHO, June 25–29, 2007, Washington, DC. See http://iris.paho.org/xmlui /bitstream/handle/123456789/5599/ce140.r13-e.pdf?sequence=1&isAllowed=y.

References

CARICOM (Caribbean Community). 2007a. "A Community for All: Declaration on Functional Cooperation." Declaration by CARICOM heads of government, Needham's Point, Barbados, July 1–4. http://www.caricom.org/jsp/communications/meetings_state-ments/declaration_on_functional_cooperation.jsp.

———. 2007b. "Declaration of Port of Spain: Uniting to Stop the Epidemic of Chronic NCDs." Special Regional Summit on Chronic Noncommunicable Diseases, Port of Spain, Trinidad and Tobago, September 15. http://www.caricom.org/jsp/communications /meetings_statements/declaration_port_of_spain_chronic_ncds.jsp.

Fifth Summit of the Americas. 2009. "Declaration of Commitment of Port of Spain." The Fifth Summit of the Americas, Port of Spain, Trinidad and Tobago, April 7–19.

Kurowski, C., C. Carpio, M. Vujicic, L. O. Gostin, and T. Baytor. 2012. *Towards a Regional Strategy to Strengthen the Nurse Workforce of the English-Speaking CARICOM:*

International Legal Instruments, Agreements and Obligations. Washington, DC: World Bank.

PAHO (Pan American Health Organization). 2011. *Human Resources for Health in the Caribbean: A Review of the Workforce Situation and the National Baselines of the 20 Goals for Human Resources for Health.* Washington, DC: PAHO.

PAHO (Pan American Health Organization) and Health Canada. 2005. "Toronto Call to Action. 2006–2015: Towards a Decade of Human Resources in Health for the Americas." Regional Meeting of the Observatory of Human Resources in Health, Toronto, October.

WHO (World Health Organization). 2006. *World Health Report 2006: Working Together for Health.* Geneva: WHO.

———. 2008. *2008–2013 Action Plan for the Global Strategy for the Prevention and Control of Noncommunicable Diseases.* Geneva: WHO.

WHO (World Health Organization) and Global Health Workforce Alliance. 2008. *The Kampala Declaration and Agenda for Global Action.* Geneva: WHO.

———. 2011. "From Kampala to Bangkok: Reviewing Progress, Renewing Commitments." Statement of the Second Global Forum on Human Resources for Health, Bangkok, January 27–29. http://www.who.int/workforcealliance/forum/2011/Outcomestatement.pdf.